IT'S NOT ALL
BLACK AND WHITE

It's Not All
Black And White

From Junior High to the Sugar Bowl, an Inside Look
at Football Through the Eyes of an Official

Mike Liner
with Doug Hensley

Skyhorse Publishing

Skyhorse Publishing books may be purchased in bulk at special discounts for sales promotion, corporate gifts, fund-raising, or educational purposes. Special editions can also be created to specifications. For details, contact the Special Sales Department, Skyhorse Publishing, 555 Eighth Avenue, Suite 903, New York, NY 10018 or info@skyhorsepublishing.com.

www.skyhorsepublishing.com

10 9 8 7 6 5 4 3 2 1

Library of Congress Cataloging-in-Publication Data

Liner, Mike.
  It's not all black and white : from junior high to the Sugar Bowl, an inside look at football through the eyes of an official / Mike Liner, with Doug Hensley.
     p. cm.
  Includes index.
  ISBN 978-1-60239-685-2 (alk. paper)
  1. Liner, Mike. 2. Football--Texas. 3. Football--Officiating--Texas. 4. Football referees--Texas--Biography. I. Hensley, Doug. II. Title.
  GV939.L57A3 2009
  796.332092--dc22
  [B]

                                    2009021846

Printed in the United States of America

For Suzie, the best call I ever made in my life.
No instant replay required.

CONTENTS

PREFACE

IT IS IMPOSSIBLE to be a successful college football official without possessing character and strong faith. Rest assured, black, dark days occur in this business. That is hard on the men who do it, and it is especially hard on the ones whose sense of identity is defined by being a college football official.

It is extremely difficult to go out on the field the next time after being chewed up and spit out over the previous week's performance.

It doesn't have to be a call that costs one team the game; it might just be a couple of critical mistakes.

I was fortunate to have a couple of anchors in my life that helped me keep everything in perspective. The first was my faith in Christ. I haven't always practiced my faith as well as I should have, but He was the rock throughout my officiating career and gave me a solid foundation for life after football when I made my decision to end my days on the field. If you hold the conviction that what you are doing is right for your life, faith will make it a much easier decision. I've tried to sprinkle in aspects of that foundation throughout this book.

The second anchor was my banking career. Gene Benham, president of First State Bank in Morton, Texas, motivated me to pursue a life in banking. One of the philosophies Mr. Benham shared with me in banking was a belief that running a bank is much like officiating. Decisions are made without time to call a committee meeting. Calls are made, and living with them is part of the game. Certainly, not every decision in the banking business is made on the fly, but it helps to be decisive. The same is true in officiating. Indecisiveness is fatal for an official.

The banking business has been good to me, and I feel fortunate to have been a part of City Bank, Texas, for so long. City Bank has been not only understanding but also encouraging about my passion for officiating. I have spent many days away from the bank over the years because of my avocation, and it has never been an issue for City Bank.

Curtis Griffith, chairman of the board of our bank, was extremely supportive of my career because he knew it would not affect my performance as CEO. City Bank grew and thrived throughout my years as both CEO and a Division I football official. The exponential growth of the bank was a result of our commitment to people inside and outside of our operation, a core belief that continues to prevail today.

I have a deep appreciation and regard for the people with whom I worked, in the bank and on the field. I like to think I did things right on the field—I missed calls, but I always tried to do the right thing—and that belief carries over into the workplace. City Bank empowers its employees to do the right thing, and then we get out of their way and let them do it.

Don't take my word for it. City Bank has been named one of the Great Places to Work in Texas by *Texas Monthly* magazine for the past three years, and we have been selected one of the top fifty small and medium-sized workplaces in America by the Great Place to Work Institute and the Society for Human Resource Management each of the past two years.

I found it interesting that as I moved up the officiating ladder and my career evolved, the bank also grew in terms of market share and visibility.

I am equally proud of each achievement.

Foreword

IT **IS DIFFICULT** to describe the level of togetherness officials develop while working on a college football crew. We look around the stadium and realize we don't have anyone on our side except those other men in striped shirts. We get a certain sense of pride from that and from being able to do something a lot of other people would like to do.

Of course, if it were easy to be a college football official, everyone would do it. Because it's not easy, that makes it very special.

Another thing that draws officials together is a sense of shared experiences, many of which Mike Liner articulates in the pages you are about to read. As Mike explains, every official starts out the same way, working youth games and moving up the ladder to more meaningful games. There are no shortcuts to the top, and everyone goes through the same drill and same basic training. By way of example, I officiated for sixteen years before working my first Division I game, and I worked for twelve years before I called a college game of any kind.

That is similar to the source of military camaraderie–shared experiences. Even though a dichotomy exists between enlisted men and officers, they have shared experiences. Moving that analogy to the world of college football officiating, everyone is a grunt at some level. The payoff, though, comes when we are privileged to walk onto the field for a Division I college football game. The atmosphere of college football is something special, and the chance to be on the field with some of the greatest players and coaches in the country is a real privilege. I can't describe it any other way.

Officials have a unique place, regardless of the sport. They represent the integrity of the game, which is why it hurts all officials when one in any sport is caught cheating. I have never minded fans objecting to judgment calls or my knowledge of the rules. That is one thing. But when they attack my integrity, that's where the line is drawn. Officials not only represent the integrity of the game. They *are* the integrity of the game.

I'm really happy Mike took the time to write a book from the official's point of view. I'm not sure people have an idea, not that they should, about what it is like to be on that field. A lot of folks think these guys in striped shirts just show up at the stadium, shake a few hands, and work a football game. But the reality is that we prepare hard, and we invest energy, intensity and passion—just like players, coaches, and fans—in a game we love.

If we're good at our job and a little bit lucky, we get a chance to work the biggest and best games. That happened to me in 1993, when Mike and I were part of the officiating crew for the national championship game between Alabama and Miami. Mike details the experience in the early pages of this book, and I can say it was the most intense three hours of my life. The atmosphere inside the Louisiana Superdome was unbelievable.

I can still remember blowing my whistle during the first five minutes of the game and being unable to hear it. During the coin toss, we were screaming at each other about calling heads or tails. As I'm sure many fans remember, that was the first time it was set up for the No. 1 team to play No. 2. It happened accidentally on previous occasions, but this time it was intentional, and it pitted two incredible programs against each other. As an aside, now that I'm in the Southeastern Conference, I've gained an even greater appreciation for the passion Alabama fans have when it comes to Crimson Tide football.

Just being selected for that game was a tremendous honor and a tremendous responsibility. It was a great game without a lot of controversy in terms of officiating. The atmosphere was unlike anything I have experienced before or since.

To give you an idea of that Crimson Tide passion I mentioned earlier, a couple of years ago I was in Birmingham when my anniversary rolled around. I called a local florist to order flowers for my wife and used a credit card to pay. The person taking my order asked what name was on the credit card, and I told her Rogers Redding. She said, "You're a football official." I was taken aback and told her that I used to be an official but was now retired.

After another long pause, she said, "You worked the 1993 national championship game." I told her I did and wondered how she would know that. "I have that game on tape and watch it three times a year," she said. Remember, this was just a few years ago, long removed from 1993. It's a real indicator of what a huge part of people's lives college football can be and a reminder that football officials are under tremendous scrutiny when a fan remembers the name of a referee from a game played fifteen years earlier.

I want to close with a few points to emphasize some of what Mike will say. Football officiating is a paid hobby. Nobody is in this as a profession. It is merely an avocation they really like tremendously. Many would do it for nothing because no one is in it to get rich. Anyone who is in it to get rich made the wrong choice because he won't. I think that's part of what makes college football such a pure and wonderful game. Could officials be paid more? No question. I'm sure every football coach would like to make more money no matter what his current salary is, but for a coach, this represents his life's work. If a football official is fired, it's not a pleasant thing, but he has another life out there. That's very different from someone who has his entire livelihood and family invested in his job.

Finally, I'd be remiss if I didn't pay homage to the Southwest Conference. When Arkansas left the SWC and it became entirely a

Texas conference, I think that gave it a family feel. There was a certain intimacy about it. However, if the SWC were still in business today, I'm certain it would have a corporate feel to it. That is partly because college football now has a greater level of scrutiny, with virtually every game televised, every play analyzed, and everyone in the bleachers holding a cell-phone camera. Throw in the Internet, where any controversial play can be posted to YouTube within thirty seconds. We didn't have that kind of scrutiny in the SWC. The league was unique in many ways, but primarily because college football was a different game in a different environment back then.

That's not to say it wasn't special. As Mike so aptly says, the life of a college football official is also special. I felt blessed to be a part of the brotherhood. I was lucky to be in the right place at the right time. Some of the best friends in my life are guys from those days.

Here's hoping you enjoy getting to know some of those guys, as well. After all, once the striped shirts come off, we're really pretty decent fellows.

— Rogers Redding
Coordinator of Football
Officials, Southeastern Conference;
Secretary-Rules Editor, NCAA
Football Rules Committee

Introduction

"The essence of sports is that while you're doing it, nothing else matters, but after you stop, there is a place, generally not very important, where you would put it."

—Roger Bannister

I **HAD ONE OF** the best seats in the house, yet almost every week I heard how I couldn't see a thing.

As it turned out, the view was fine, but I had lost sight of some of the more important things in life. College football is a great game, a pure game and a beautiful game, but that is all it is—a game played across the country by young men on autumn Saturdays.

As a college football official, I had, quite literally, a sideline view of the game's greatest players and coaches for nearly twenty years.

Working a football game requires much more than showing up a few minutes before kickoff, shaking a few hands, and making sure you have one of those cool yellow handkerchiefs in your pocket.

It is a week of preparation followed by a weekend of focused work, and if you are not ready by the opening kickoff, it won't be long before the crowd knows it—and lets you know it.

For me, those weekends stacked up for a long time, and they got in the way of some other important aspects of my life: service and worship. It doesn't take much for a wedge to be driven into your spiritual walk, no matter where you are along the way. Sometimes, the smallest things become a wedge. Other times, the things you love can become the wedge.

Don't be fooled. Officiating is hard work, and the men you see on television every weekend make it look easy because they prepare hard the other six days of the week. Officiating is an avocation, and the only way to become proficient enough to work at the highest levels is to work as often as you can.

That's how something you love can get in the way of something more important, and that's where I found myself not too long ago. I had been like any other official, toiling to improve over the years, and I was drawn to the excitement that comes with working bigger, better games. The difference between working a Lone Star Conference game in Edmond, Oklahoma, and working a Big 12 Conference game in Norman, Oklahoma, is huge. I'm not taking anything away from the Lone Star Conference; I worked plenty of games in that league, too. But stepping onto a field to officiate a nationally televised game between two traditional powers led by high-profile coaches with 80,000 people in attendance is indescribable.

That makes it easy to get caught up in the reality of the human condition. Traveling that path—and we've all been on it at one time or another for different lengths of time—tends to keep you from focusing on your faith. Some people out there can do both, but more probably struggle doing both. As a football official, I was traveling on the weekends, spending time studying the rulebook and preparing for the next game during the week instead of reading a Sunday school lesson or a daily Bible study. For me, the result was a slow and steady falling away from my faith.

That was my routine from late August to early December each year for a very long time. Spending so much time concentrating on little besides football can cause one to lose his place on his spiritual walk.

I needed to find my place, and more importantly, I wanted to find my place. I had officiated football games for thirty-five years and had been part of the Big 12 officiating group since the conference was formed in 1996.

Internally, knowing when it was time to retire was one of my biggest worries. Every year, someone hung it up and someone new came in. Between the guys calling it quits and the guys breaking in, you could always find a couple of guys who had stayed too long. They were no longer at the peak of their game. They were the guys who didn't receive a bowl game assignment at the end of the season because their weekly game grades were too low. Gradually, they lost the admiration of the other guys in the league, and they never gained the respect of the new officials coming in because the new guys didn't get to see them in their prime.

I didn't want to be a member of that not-so-proud fraternity. I don't know how it works for everyone, but I knew when the time had come for me to start thinking about retirement. I was almost sixty years old. When I was fifty-five or fifty-six, I started thinking about it. When I turned fifty-seven and officiating suddenly wasn't as much fun as it had been, I knew the time to retire was approaching.

I dreaded going to the airport, dreaded going to bad hotels. I didn't spend as much time the week before preparing for a three-hour-plus game. The stadiums were the same old stadiums I had been going to for years. I had worked virtually every combination of Big 12 games possible, and it was just not as enjoyable as it used to be for me.

What I did look forward to was being assigned to a good bowl game, but having already worked a lot of those, it was easy to lose the drive and focus that I possessed earlier in my career. That happens everywhere in sports—to professional and college players alike—if they are not hungry. It's hard enough to reach the pinnacle, and much harder to stay there, if that hunger is gone. It's a natural thing; it becomes more and more difficult to find the motivation. The only real motivation left after almost twenty years of officiating Division

I football was realizing that my performance would be graded at the end of the year.

If there are six or seven line judges in the league, none of them wants to be graded fifth, sixth, or seventh. Each wants to be in the top three. The grading system is such that practically no difference can be found in the top four, but if you finish third, you will be assigned to a third-tier bowl rather than a top bowl, and that's the motivation.

So as I approached that time in my life, I started considering how important it had become to exit gracefully on my own terms. As I did that, I realized I had put my faith on the back burner for a long time and that I had not served the Lord in the way I knew in my heart I was supposed to be doing. I prayed about it a lot, and when the time came, I knew it was time. I am not a theologian by any stretch of the imagination, but I knew it was time, and I knew I wanted to end my officiating career on my own terms because of all the things I was missing in my life.

I wanted to quit while I was still respected by my peers and by coaches, and I wanted to go out feeling like I was at the top of my game. Too many officials do not leave the Division I level like that because that position is such a high for them. It becomes their identity. It is who they are, not what they do, and that is a hard line to walk. People talk to me today, and if the subject of football officiating comes up, they are interested in what it's like to be a football official. They don't even acknowledge this other life I lead that involves being CEO of a bank. To many of them, my work at the bank is what I do on the side.

Life is about so much more.

After so many years of trying to figure out the best way to get from Lubbock, Texas, to Lincoln, Nebraska, and back, making hotel and rental car reservations, making arrangements to leave work Friday, and packing bags every week, it began to wear on me. To people who travel all the time, that might not seem like a big deal, but after years of that routine, week after week and year after year, it became tedious for me.

Beyond that, it's easy to fall into a trap. If I was assigned to a low-profile, late season game in which nothing was on the line and virtually everyone in the conference and country was focused on other games, it was easy for my concentration to wane.

The cure for that is to get out on the field and expect it to be a great game from the first play. Remember how important it is to the players and the coaches. Remember how far fans drove to sit in the stands and watch. All of those people are doing their jobs, and the officials have to do their jobs, too. That said, the process, from start to finish, can be a real grind.

The realization struck home that it was time for me to step aside. I knew it would be tough to turn my back on the game and walk away, but I had no idea just how hard it was going to be. The fact hit me hardest when that first summer rolled around and I was no longer working Big 12 games. I missed the camaraderie of the officiating brotherhood as well as all the off season and preseason meetings we go through to get ready for the next season. Even though it felt like drudgery at times when I was doing it, I missed it.

Something true in all sports is equally true in officiating: Youth is served. There might be something to be said for having experience and being in the top echelon among your peers, but at some point, the new guys come in, and the old guys must move aside. It was important to me to leave before I felt like I was being pushed out. The rules of life in general and sports in particular dictate with ruthless inevitability that youth must and will be served.

Often, older guys are out there officiating who probably don't need to be there. When I first got into college football officiating with the Southwest Conference at age forty, the mandatory retirement age in the league was sixty. At age forty, twenty years seems like an eternity. The truth is that guys who stay past sixty are only kidding themselves. I left at fifty-eight before I fooled myself into believing that I was still competing at the high level demanded of officials in the Big 12 Conference.

For me, the beginning of the end came in the summer of 2005, when I made the decision to step aside as the season was approaching. The Big 12 had its summer meeting for officials at the University of Kansas that year, and we had spent four days in Lawrence, Kansas, studying rules changes, sitting in meetings, and reviewing training tapes. All of this takes place indoors. We also have outdoor training, where we go through agility drills and other requirements such as running a mile within a certain time. The league wants to make sure officials are taking care of themselves and staying in shape. It isn't rigorous, but it was the eighteenth time I'd been through it, and I knew with certainty that I wasn't enjoying it. None of my officiating responsibilities were as exciting as they had once been. Based on that, I knew it was a good time to retire. I called Tim Millis, the supervisor of officials, and told him that 2005 was going to be my last season. I didn't expect anyone's pity, breaks on game grades, or great game assignments. He deserved to know in case he had a particular line judge in mind that he wanted to scout to take my spot on my crew.

I had no plans to announce the decision to my fellow officials. I just wanted to go through the season and work my usual way without any rhetoric about it being my last time to do all the things we do each season. I wanted to go through that myself and deal with it in my own way. Eventually, other officials figured it out, and toward the latter part of the season I told some of them. I even worked with a couple of different crews toward the end of the season. I think Tim made those assignments on purpose because he knew I wanted to work with specific guys and some wanted to work with me before the end. My schedule was pretty good; I had some of the better games that year, even though I had not asked for them.

One of those great games was the very last one I worked, the annual clash between Oklahoma State and Oklahoma. The game featured two coaches I have tremendous admiration for: Bob Stoops of Oklahoma and Les Miles, who was then the head coach of the

Cowboys. Each game, the line judge and the field judge go out on the field one hour before kickoff. That's something I always looked forward to. Coach Stoops and I have always had this deal where once he is through talking to the opposing coach, he would come by and chat with me. He came over that day, and I told him it was my last time to work his sideline.

He gave me a funny look and asked why. That helped me to realize I had made a great decision, because it confirmed to me that I was walking away at the top of my game. I had and still have ultimate admiration for Coach Stoops, and if he thought my abilities as an official had diminished he would have encouraged me to retire instead of questioning my decision.

You can go on and on about all the things Coach Stoops does right with his football program. If something goes wrong, he steps up and takes responsibility. He is organized. He cares about the fact that he puts good players on the field, and they put a good product on the field. Oklahoma is a top-notch program. He has some of the same off-the-field problems as anyone else, and they get magnified a little more because of the microscope he is under at one of the premier programs in the nation. By the same token, when he has a call go against him, you never hear him criticize the officials. He knows that is part of the game.

If I had an opportunity that final season, I took a moment and told coaches I knew well enough of my retirement plans. Bill Snyder at Kansas State was one of those. The last game I ever worked for him was at Iowa State. Near the end of the game, when he wasn't coaching, I went up to him and told him how much respect and admiration I had for him. I told him I was retiring and that I really enjoyed working his games. He took off his headset and couldn't say a word. What I didn't know at the time was that he had made the same decision but had not yet announced it. When he did make his retirement official a short time later, I thought back to that conversation and knew he had something he wanted to tell me, but it just wouldn't come out. Coaches handle things different ways, and Coach Snyder's way was to wait until the season was over to make his retirement plans public.

At that final Oklahoma State–Oklahoma game, Coach Stoops decided to give me a going-away party of sorts. He was animated on the sidelines throughout the game, but I knew him well enough to know at least some of it was in jest. The OU–Oklahoma State game is an intense rivalry, and this one came just a week after a very controversial Texas Tech–OU game in which Tech had won in Lubbock on the game's last play. Needless to say, the fans at OU were still irate because of their perception that the officials had robbed them on several occasions in that game.

Those fans were still in a bad mood when it came to anyone walking around wearing black and white stripes. We were on the field before the game looking things over, and the fans were really letting us have it. One fan in the front row hollered and wanted to know if any of us blankety-blanks were from Lubbock, Texas, and hey, it was my last game, so I was feeling pretty spunky. I didn't have to worry about getting fired over jawing with a fan, so I had no problem letting him know that's where I lived. Of course, that really set him off.

As for the game itself, Oklahoma got the better of its in-state rival most of the game, but the Sooners also had a number of holding calls go against them in the first half. Stoops was having an ongoing discussion with me about those calls, but it was pretty tame stuff—a typical give-and-take.

When halftime arrived, we headed for the officials' locker room, and to get there we had to walk through a small opening and travel a good distance. Officials receive a police escort, but they are still moving among fans. We encountered a guy with a tray full of soft drinks and popcorn, and he started verbally harassing us with some pretty rough language. The police officer looked at us and asked if we wanted him to get rid of the guy. Of course, we said yes, and the officer escorted the fan out of the stadium. In fact, he brought the guy's ticket stub to our dressing room and said that fan wouldn't be returning. He got what he deserved, and I'm sure he was outside the stadium calling his wife on his cell phone, saying something like, "Honey, you're probably wondering where the heck I am. You'll never guess what happened on the way back from the concession stand."

Once that excitement subsided, we returned for the second half, and Stoops was continuing to harass me about the holding calls, wondering very loudly if it we'd help set a school record for holding calls against his team that day. While he was complaining, I threw a flag on the Sooners' left tackle for a holding call a blind man could have made. Stoops saw it and took off down the sidelines to get away from me to keep from having to admit I was right. I was laughing. One of his assistants was laughing because Stoops took off. It was an obvious call, and the game was in hand. Stoops wouldn't even look my way the rest of the game.

Moments like that made me love being a college football official. The memories. The people. The games. The calls. It is a ride very few people get to take, and it is my pleasure to share that ride with you.

It is my hope this book gives you an inside view of what it looks like from one of the best—and toughest—seats in the house.

IT'S NOT ALL
BLACK AND WHITE

CHAPTER ONE:
WELCOME TO THE BIG TIME

"If you want to walk the heavenly streets of gold, you gotta know the password, 'Roll, Tide, Roll!'"

—Paul "Bear" Bryant, former head coach,

University of Alabama

YOU DON'T SUDDENLY wind up on the floor of the Superdome as an official in the national championship game. It takes time, hard work, and perseverance. As far as my officiating career is concerned, January 1, 1993, will always represent one of the great blessings in my life—the hand of God providing a good opportunity and a great privilege.

Many officials work their entire careers and never receive a chance to experience the unique atmosphere of a national championship game. For me, it happened after my fourth full season in the Southwest Conference. I was a relative newcomer to the SWC, working a mere three games in 1988 before being assigned a full schedule the next four seasons.

After the 1992 regular season concluded, I was the line judge assigned to the Sugar Bowl. Certainly, I was not the most experienced line judge they could have selected, but I had a good year on the field and felt like I was capable of doing as good a job as anyone else.

I could not have found out about the assignment at a better time. My father was in an Amarillo hospital fighting colon cancer. In fact, he'd lost part of his colon, and he was in very serious condition because of complications following surgery. I was staying with him that week when my cell phone rang, and Wendell Shelton, the SWC supervisor of officials, told me I had been selected to work the big game.

Receiving the news from Wendell was nice because he was the referee on my first Southwest Conference crew. I worked with him the better part of four years, and he and his wife, Peggy, have been longtime friends of mine.

It was only the second week of December, which meant I had plenty of time to get ready. Really, the assignment was a blessing because I was rather depressed at that point in my life. I didn't know if my father was going to make it. To get the assignment when I did was quite uplifting and gave me something to look forward to. The fact that my father battled through the complications and is still alive fifteen years later only made everything more satisfying.

As it happened, I was going to be part of a great crew. Gary Slaughter, the head linesman, had been in the league one year less than I had. Jon Bible, the field judge, and Rogers Redding, the referee, were also selected. It was particularly gratifying for me to see Jon and Rogers on the crew because all three of us entered the league together. I like to think of that time as a strong recruiting year for SWC officials. Both Jon and Rogers went on to become very good officials.

Gary Slaughter, meanwhile, moved on to the National Football League and worked several Super Bowls. Joe Darden, the umpire on our crew, had a great reputation for excellence. He was the premier umpire in the SWC at that time. Ron Murphy, the back judge, had worked in the NFL for a few years before returning to the college level, and side judge Mike Wetzel had been around for years. Joe, Ron, and Mike all had experience officiating national championship games.

We had four highly experienced officials and two more that were absolutely brilliant in their knowledge of the rules. Rogers is one of the best football rules guys around. You always need someone like that on your crew because you never know what might occur on the field. It was the perfect mix of experienced men and guys who were less seasoned but had earned the opportunity. Youth was being served.

The game was played on a Friday night, and the league wanted us there two days early. We checked in at the Hyatt Regency, which is basically right across the street from the Superdome. After we arrived and settled in, we spent some time enjoying New Orleans and took in Pete Fountain's show at the Hilton that first night.

The fun ended at 9 AM the next day. That's when the Sugar Bowl conference was scheduled. It's a meeting that includes coaches, television people, Sugar Bowl staff, representatives from the participating universities and the conference they represented, and us, the game officials.

We walked into this big meeting room at the Superdome and saw a podium at the front of the room with tables on each side facing the audience. Coach Gene Stallings, Alabama people, and SEC folks were seated at one table, and Coach Dennis Erickson, his athletic director, and Miami people were at the other. The room was full of media, and the man speaking at the front of the room was the director of operations for the Sugar Bowl.

I will never forget the seven of us walking in and sitting in chairs at the back of the room. The Sugar Bowl official asked everyone around the room to introduce themselves so everyone knew who was there and what their responsibilities would be. Gene Stallings introduced himself. All the Alabama people introduced themselves. Television sportscaster Brent Musburger introduced himself. Finally, we got to the back row, and I stood up and said, "I'm Mike Liner, Southwest Conference line judge."

That got everyone's attention. Hearing someone announce they were from the Southwest Conference was like someone saying they'd just flown in from Cuba. In a matter of moments, everyone had turned around because they wanted a good, hard look at this group of people from the SWC. The meeting continued. They asked Rogers a question or two. The producer told everyone how many television timeouts per quarter there would be, how long those timeouts would last, all the typical issues associated with a big-time college football television production.

When the meeting concluded, there came Gene Stallings right up the center aisle, right to me. He looked me in the eye and said, "Since you are the line judge, I just want you to know they call me 'Jolly Gene' on the sideline." I'm thinking, "Sure, they do." At the time, I didn't know any SEC officials to confirm this new and friendly attitude, but my experience with coaches has been that if they make a point of telling you how easy they are to get along with, they generally turn out to be pretty vocal during the game. This time was no exception.

After the meeting, we returned to the hotel. We were on the elevator, riding up with some of the guys from the ESPN GameDay crew. Turns out they were staying on our floor. We had all seen those guys on television before. I have to tell you, for a boy from Morton, Texas, I had to pinch myself and ask, "What am I doing here?" Before I'd left Texas, I'd seen stories about me working the game in the local newspapers. It was no secret among the local football official chapters in the West Texas towns of Lubbock, Amarillo, Midland, Odessa, and Abilene. Everybody was going to know about an area official working a game of this magnitude.

The pressure was beginning to mount on me. The people in my hometown were talking to me about it. People are people, and they like to see someone they know in this kind of situation. Of course, human nature being what it is, your mind starts to wonder: Are they watching the race or waiting for a car wreck? Those are the kinds of things that go through your mind.

Morton, Texas, is a town of only 2,000 people, and I was the bank president. I had officiated high school games with a lot of guys over the years, and in officiating circles, you will always have rules guys. They are the guys who not only know the rules, but the exceptions to every one. This is especially true at the high school level. So, when these guys are watching a game, they aren't really watching the game as much as they're watching the officials. From the standpoint of my fellow officials, I knew I was being looked at with many a critical eye.

I was representing the Southwest Conference, and I did not want to do anything to discredit officiating in my league. Anytime you step out on the field as an official, you put your credibility and self-esteem on the line. If you do something wrong out there—such as miss a simple offsides call—you open yourself up to a lot of second-guessing. When you are in the crucible of the national championship game, you'd better believe that pressure will find you from every direction. However, I believe most of the pressure a football official feels is self-imposed.

Remember the original purpose of bowl games? They were designed to be a reward for players and fans. Sure, every team wants to win. No one wants to get blown out on national television, but by and large, they are built for fun. The system we have now includes more than thirty bowl games, yet only one of them truly matters.

One. And game officials are squarely in the cross-hairs of pressure. The conference supervisor of officials will be there, and he expects the officials in his charge to represent the league well and call the game correctly. Fellow Southwest Conference officials are sitting at home watching with a critical eye, questioning why they are not there themselves. Those guys are really paying attention. I was so young and inexperienced at that point in my career that it was an instance where being dumb was a good thing. It's possible not to realize one's shortcomings until much later, after addressing and working on them.

I bet Coach Stallings saw those shortcomings, though. A few years later, Alabama produced a tape of its greatest games, and of course that Sugar Bowl victory was among them. I watched the tape and spent a lot of time watching my mechanics. How I compared mechanically in 1993 with 2005 was dramatically different—and not in a positive way. When it's the national championship game, which is supposed to be the best of the best, you only want the best on the field. A few years later, when the Big 12 Conference came along, training for officials improved exponentially. That wasn't necessarily the case at that time in the SWC.

Conference personnel believed in picking guys out of the high school and small college ranks, and they learned officiating by working with conference veterans. I started studying officiating on television more intensely when I got to the college level. That was when I made it my business to watch every college football game I could. Of course, there weren't nearly as many televised games two decades ago as there are today.

Finally, game day rolled around. It was a night game in New Orleans, which is something special in itself. We started our pregame preparation routine early that morning, broke for lunch, and then continued our pregame. We left for the stadium around 4 PM. At this point, all we wanted to do was get to the stadium. We broke, got to our rooms, collected our bags, got our ties on, and prepared to leave.

With kickoff nearing, the city was officially bananas. The Hyatt was also the headquarters for Alabama's fans, which added to the highly charged atmosphere. You could not go anywhere in the hotel without fighting through a loud, boisterous crowd. We were standing around waiting for an elevator so we could get our bags and return to the lobby and leave. The lobby was absolute chaos. We were trying to get together so we could travel together to the stadium, but it was virtually impossible. We finally reached the front door and walked across the street, and it was still wall-to-wall people. Our short walk was nothing but being part of a mass of humanity all trying to reach the same place. We were accustomed to traveling to stadiums, entering through the back gate, and having the police meet us to show us our dressing room.

This was not the case today.

When we arrived at the stadium, we didn't have tickets. We had to spend a few minutes convincing the guy at the turnstile that we really were the game officials. While this discussion was taking place, we were holding up the line. The game was still hours away, but the Superdome was already a circus.

Fans might think the officials for the biggest college football game in America would have someone taking care of them, making sure they got where they were supposed to when they needed to be there. In this case, that was not even close to being true. None of us had a clue about the Superdome. We didn't know the ins and outs. Talk about going with the flow. We got into the stadium, took an elevator to a tunnel and walked around to our dressing room. At last.

Once we got settled in, it was the same pregame routine for us as it was for our final regular season game. We did the same things. The only difference was this one had more media focus. The number of players, the field, and the professional relationships were all the same. I knew what to expect working that sideline.

But make no mistake, I knew it was the big time. Brent Musburger, the great longtime broadcaster, has a habit of coming by the officials' dressing room and visiting with the officials before the game. He was at the Sugar Bowl that night, and I have had the chance to visit with him many times since. When he is present, it gives the perspective of a big-time football game for which I had an incredible view. Arguably the best in the house.

After meeting with Musburger, we got dressed and headed out onto the field. It was easily the biggest crowd I had ever seen. Part of my duty that night was to bring Alabama onto the field. Let me tell you, the Crimson Tide was ready to rumble. I walked down the hallway and turned the corner toward their dressing room, and the Alabama players started running out of there. I'd been around a lot of football teams, but I had never seen one pumped up like Alabama was that night. I thought I was going to get run over and hurt before the game even began.

The Miami team featured Heisman Trophy–winner Gino Torretta at quarterback. I was thinking I would be working the losing sideline because the Hurricanes were such a heavy favorite, but when those Tide players came running through the tunnel like that, it was my first clue Alabama just might win this game.

We didn't throw many flags that night, but each one of the thirteen we threw (six against the Hurricanes, seven against the Tide) created plenty of buzz. The historic Alabama program was in search of its twelfth national championship, but it was an eight-and-a-half-point underdog to Miami, which had won twenty-nine consecutive games heading into the Sugar Bowl, including the previous season's national championship game.

As is usually the case, at least one of our calls created controversy. Early in the game, Alabama broke a play to Miami's one-yard line, and as running back Derrick Lassic got up after being tackled, he spun the ball on the field like a top.

Well, that kind of showmanship was not tolerated. Football is and always will be a team sport, and anything that draws attention to an individual doesn't reflect the sportsmanship the NCAA wants demonstrated. The rule book is also clear on this issue. Our crew spent time talking about what had happened, and the rule dictates that the ball should either be handed to an official or left at the spot. You won't find anything in there about spiking it, slamming it, spinning it, or performing any other extracurricular activities with the football at the end of a play. Those things are considered unsportsmanlike.

The player spun the ball. Ron Murphy, the back judge, was standing on the goal line, and he had a clear look at the showboating. He threw a flag for a fifteen-yard unsportsmanlike conduct penalty. Instead of first-and-goal at the one, Alabama had it first-and-goal at the sixteen. It was my unpleasant duty to report the infraction to "Jolly Gene" on the Alabama sideline. To say that Stallings was disappointed by the call would be a dramatic understatement.

He was on my case for the rest of the game, even though Alabama won going away, 34–13.

The Superdome crowd was so loud that I could see Coach Stallings screaming at me, but I could not hear him. It was the loudest environment I had ever experienced in my life. The place was packed. The crowd was oiled up. It was a huge 'Bama crowd.

We had at least one other memorable call besides that one unsportsmanlike conduct. On one play, Torretta completed a long pass down the sideline opposite from me. Miami receiver Lamar Thomas was moving toward the goal line when an Alabama defensive back George Teague came up from behind and stripped the ball away, but by the time the defensive player could stop his momentum and turn around, he was in his own end zone. A safety was now possible, but he came out of the end zone and ran it all the way back into Miami territory. It was a great play and a potential momentum-shifter.

There was one problem, though. I had an Alabama defensive player offsides at the snap. If you think Coach Stallings was displeased with the unsportsmanlike conduct call, he was even less impressed with this one. It was one of the few chinks in the Tide's armor that night. Talk about superior game planning and execution. It was an inspired effort in a great college football environment. It's not often that an underdog of that magnitude prevails by three touchdowns in a national championship setting.

As the game was wrapping up and the clock was ticking down, I remember that Coach Stallings had screamed at me and his players so often that he had just about lost his voice. His volume was dialed down by about ninety percent. I jokingly asked him if he'd lost his voice, but he didn't really see the humor in that.

Alabama scored twice within sixteen seconds in the third quarter, essentially securing the game. The Tide's defense played tremendously as well. In John Copeland and Eric Curry they had two of the best defensive ends in the country and an athletic secondary, and their athletes just dominated. Can you imagine what kind of pressure Coach Stallings was under? There he was at one of the most storied programs in the country, coaching in Bear Bryant's shadow, hearing a lot of people tell him he wasn't enough of a coach to carry Bear's suitcase. But he went in there, put together an immensely talented team—the kind that can compete at the highest level—and crushed the defending champs. His players were not the least bit intimidated by the Miami mystique. In fact, it might have been the other way around. The Tide played smash-mouth football, and a lot of Miami's taunting and trash talk vanished after they got hit in the mouth a few times.

Considering the stage, it was a cleanly played game. It was one of those games where you just put the ball down, stand back, let the players play and officiate the obvious things. That's how all the big games should be. Occasionally, it can't be that way because officials have to break up players taunting each other or maybe sting a couple of defensive backs early to leave the receivers alone or give a sideline warning. None of that came up in this game. It was just two good teams playing football. I've had a number of games like that, but I've also had them the other way when you have to be more involved in certain aspects of the game than you would like.

In a championship setting, you have to give the coaches a lot of leeway when it comes to what they say. I knew the pressure I was feeling, and I can't imagine what it was like for the two coaches. Miami, the defending national champion, is expected to win. Alabama is Alabama, and the Tide was hungry on this night. After being around those Alabama folks a few days, I got a sense of the pride they have in that program. They are the same kind of great people found at virtually every superior program. With the massive expectations heaped onto the shoulders of both coaches, we linesmen are more likely to tolerate a little more abuse from them than usual.

When it came to evaluating my performance in the game, the only people I cared about having respect for my work on the field were my fellow officials. If I officiated a good game, they'd know that. If I'd had a couple of tough calls or missed something, they'd know that, too. When officials come off the field, we all know who has had a good game and who hasn't. And I'm proud to say we all had a good game that night in the Sugar Bowl. We didn't have any controversial fumble calls, and we got the big stuff right.

I knew officiating a national championship game was something I might never have an opportunity to do again. It's as rare as getting struck by lightning, so I did my best to enjoy it. Officials who have worked more than one are very fortunate. Conferences are assigned bowl games on a rotating basis, and officials are assigned bowl games based upon their performance that season. A lot of stars have to line up. It has to be the year your conference is going to a particular bowl, and that bowl happens to be the national title game. What are the chances that will happen once? The bottom line, at least from an official's viewpoint, has to be that every game is just another game. I think that's the way we have to look at it for a couple of reasons—to keep the game in perspective and to keep the pressure under control.

I had also been taught early on in my officiating career to get my tail off the field once the game ended. So the minute the clock read 00:00 in the Sugar Bowl, I ran as hard as I could for the dressing room. Because of that, I missed the opportunity to soak in the postgame atmosphere that makes college football so special. Officials are not and cannot be part of the pregame hype or postgame celebration.

After the game, we went through our regular routine. We went back to the hotel and filled out the game reports that are turned into the conference. It's more of a formality for a bowl game, but it has to be done. We're just like any of the players or coaches involved. It's a relief that the game's behind us, and we can't help but wonder how history will perceive us, whether we handled every situation in the manner it should have been handled for a game of that importance. Sadly, though, the season was over, and that always left me with a big empty spot. I felt it more that year than practically any other thanks to the blessing of officiating at college football's highest level.

It was the only game in America that night, and we were the only college football officials not sitting home watching it.

That's hard to beat.

What's the Call?

Team A punts the ball. Team B's deep receiver, standing on his five-yard line, retreats and catches the kick in his end zone. He fumbles and in attempting to recover the ball, it goes out of bounds behind his own goal line. What is the ruling?

A. Safety, award two points to Team A.

B. Touchback, Team B ball first and ten at its own twenty.

C. Team A re-kicks from previous spot.

(See page 196 for answer.)

CHAPTER TWO:
THE ROAD TO DIVISION I

"The trouble with referees is that they just don't care which side wins."

— Tom Canterbury

LOVE FOOTBALL. Always have. It's a wonderful game and is particularly special to those of us who call Texas home. Whether you live in a large city or a small town, football is a big deal down here.

I was not born with the tools to be an outstanding player, although that failed to diminish my passion. I grew up during the 1950s and

'60s in Memphis, a small West Texas town. Football was the focus of the community where I was raised. I grew up wanting to play on the varsity football team after having started playing in the seventh grade.

I liked the game and understood the game. It just kind of clicked for me. I played and lettered three years and was around some great high school coaches such as Charlie Chambless and Bert Glasscock. Neither ever won a state championship, but their influence as far as teaching me an appreciation for the game was incredible.

I was a senior in 1966, the year Memphis integrated. Our football team that year would have struggled had it not been for integration, and we never had one ounce of trouble during that time. A common love of football helped bridge the gap, another reason I love the game.

So, when you have great passion but few tools, you figure out a way to stay connected to something you love. For me, that turned out to be officiating.

I was back in Memphis after graduating from Southwestern Oklahoma State, waiting to see if I had passed my pharmacy license examination, when two or three events occurred that really piqued my interest in officiating football. First, a fellow named Tony Pounds, who was a Memphis quarterback my senior year, went on to play for Oklahoma State and was splitting time at quarterback. His parents still lived in Memphis and regularly came into the drugstore where I worked. They came in one day and told me Tony was going to start for Oklahoma State in its game against Oklahoma, so we loaded up the station wagon and drove 250 miles to Norman.

I watched not only Tony, but also the officials, and I was fascinated by their role in the game. Little did I know at the time that, decades later, the final college football game I would ever work would be an Oklahoma–Oklahoma State game played in that very same stadium. That was no coincidence; I believe it was the Lord putting me where I needed to be when I needed to be there.

The next thing was I had an opportunity to officiate junior high and JV games in Memphis with a few local guys who were not regular officials. Barry Ward was a member of the officials' chapter in nearby Childress, Texas. He was a practicing official who went to meetings, took the test, and had the uniform. He had two or three of his buddies, including Terry and Gayle Monzingo, who would help him officiate the junior high games. Gayle is the father of Matt Monzingo, who would later become head coach at Memphis and take the Cyclones to a Class 1A state championship in 1991.

One week during the 1971 season, one of the guys couldn't work a game, so Barry asked me to help. He knew I loved the game. He told me, "Be the umpire. Spot the ball, watch for holding on the line, and try not to get killed."

He gave me a shirt and a red flag, which I still have. That small taste was all I needed. I was in love with officiating. It was the most exciting thing I had done since playing.

The next event occurred while my brother was still playing high school football his senior year. Memphis was contending for a district championship, and the Cyclones were going to play McLean, whose quarterback, Tommy Duniven, later went on to great success at Texas Tech.

During the game I looked down at the sideline and happened to notice that my cousin, Danny Martin, was the head linesman on the officiating crew. At that time, he was a high school science teacher in nearby Shamrock, Texas.

I had no idea he was going to officiate, and I was thinking how much I would love the opportunity to do that, too. Being a typical fan that day, I was watching my brother play and bragging that my cousin was the head linesman. As it turned out, he made a couple of calls the Memphis faithful didn't agree with, so the fans were not impressed with my cousin. McLean won the game, and I learned a lesson—keep quiet about knowing an official.

A few years later, after passing my pharmacy exam, I moved to Morton and bought my own pharmacy. In no time, I was spending twelve to fourteen hours each day working indoors. I had a young family and a new business, all the while terribly missing officiating. I woke up one day and realized that the only thing I was doing in life was spending all my time in a drugstore. I didn't have time for hobbies like golf, hunting, or fishing. I wasn't doing anything beyond work.

One day, Joe Coffman, a friend of mine, came by the drugstore and said he was planning to join the Lubbock chapter of football officials so that he could work junior high games. He invited me to go with him. It was something I wanted to do. I could start taking off Thursday afternoons to officiate games and then return to the job and finish filling prescriptions.

I went with him, joined the chapter, got the rule book, took the test, and became a member of the South Plains Football Officials Association. This organization was a part of the Southwest Football Officials Association that later became the Texas Association of Sports Officials. Joe and I became close friends and worked junior high and junior varsity games in Morton. We took turns as referee and had a three-man crew that was rounded out most of the time by Richard Houston, the junior high principal. If we could find a fourth guy to help us with the JV games, we considered that a full crew. In reality, we weren't very good, but we steadily improved.

I had no aspirations at that time to do anything beyond learning the rules so I could work those lower-level games in my hometown, but I received a chance to work my first high school game about midseason.

Ronnie Freeman was the chapter secretary, and he was responsible for making sure officiating crews were assigned. He called me one Monday morning and said he needed me to work a high school game that Friday night because one of the officials scheduled to work had a conflict. I was really excited to work a varsity game and told him so.

"We need you to go to the Cotton Center–Grady game," he said.

"That's a six-man game," I said. "I've never even seen a six-man game."

For those unfamiliar with six-man football, it has its own classification and is played by schools with the smallest enrollments in the state. Six-man football has eleven different rules. Although I knew what they were, I had never worked such a game. I was still grappling with this when he told me he needed me to work as referee. I had expected to be the head linesman.

"You have the six-man rules, and you've been refereeing games over there in Morton, so you know how," he said. "Don't worry about it. You'll be fine."

It was an atmosphere unlike anything I'd ever seen before. It was cold. The national anthem played on a record player over the loudspeaker, and most of the fans just pulled up near the unfenced field to watch the game from the warmth of their automobiles.

Still, no matter how cold it was, it was a varsity game, and I was excited to be there. We had a three-man crew, and on the first play after the opening kickoff, we marked the ball ready for play. Grady broke the huddle and came to the line.

The way they snapped the ball was one of the funniest parts of the entire game. Remember the rules differences I mentioned? Well, one stipulates the quarterback can only throw a forward pass if he takes a direct snap from center, but he can run or pass if he has a clear exchange with another back.

Here's how it worked: Grady's quarterback would line up butt-to-butt with the center and take the snap while facing the backfield. He then pitched the ball from between his legs to the fullback, and the fullback pitched it back to him. This all took place in about one second. Now, the quarterback could run or pass.

Never in my life had I seen this type of alignment between a quarterback and center, and I was thinking, "This cannot be legal." As a relatively new official, my approach was to see if anyone screamed or hollered about the play. If not, I figured they knew something about the six-man game that I was yet to learn. If there was a bunch of screaming, I would tell the offense not to do it anymore. In this case, no one screamed so I assumed it had to be legal.

There was one other interesting thing about the rules at the little stadium on that chilly, wind-blown night. Six-man football reverses extra-point conversions. Successful kicks are worth two points, and successful run or pass plays are worth one point. That's because the mechanics of snapping the ball to a holder, the handler catching the snap and placing the ball down correctly, and a kicker kicking it through the uprights, are difficult at all levels of the high school game—and particularly difficult in six-man, where it's easier and simpler to just run the ball.

Almost every time one of the teams scored, we had a point-after kick, and that kick would travel into an unlit cotton field. Ball boys were unheard of at that level. Retrieving the ball was our job, so the umpire would position himself beneath the goalpost and rule if the kick was good or not, and then he would go hunt down the ball, and we'd have to wait on him to get back.

After that first foray into the world of six-man football, my varsity schedule from the chapter included a good number of six-man games. That's how you work your way up, particularly in West Texas, which is home to many six-man schools. In this part of the world, that was the indoctrination, although that's not true today because of the tremendous shortage of football officials at the high school level.

Eventually, I did receive the opportunity to work on some four-man crews in eleven-man football. I soaked up a lot of knowledge and was determined to improve and wanted to work as many games as I could.

When I got my first Friday night varsity eleven-man game, I thought I had finally arrived. The first one I worked was Tulia at Lubbock Christian—a fairly mundane game—but it was part of how officials progressed. The football world was not focused on that game that particular week, but it was the biggest game of my officiating career to date. And like all games, it also meant a lot to the game's participants.

The South Plains chapter is a large organization made up mostly of officials from Lubbock, although some, like me, were from surrounding towns. For me, it was a 120-mile round trip each Monday night for the rules meetings. I was a regular. Regular? Heck, I never missed one. If I had been as regular a church member as I was a member of that football officiating chapter and spent as much time studying the Bible as the rules book, I would have been a much better individual. That's what I spent my time doing. In retrospect, I don't regret the football, but I do regret letting other things slide.

Chapter officials receive their schedule of games in the summer, and the rule in that chapter is unless your wife dies or you die, you need to be at every game. It takes a high level of commitment to tell someone in July that you will be there, without fail, for eleven consecutive Friday nights in the fall. We learn this at the high school level. We commit to taking a ten- or eleven-game schedule and fulfilling it every week. That way, if you are fortunate enough to move to the next level, you have established a reputation of consistency and commitment.

Football coaches decide in advance which crew will work their game because they must agree on the crew at the high school level. If Odessa Permian is playing San Angelo Central, the coaches have to agree on the officials. They won't tolerate having a Lubbock crew without knowing precisely who is on that crew and the experience level of each crew member.

The chapter secretary takes the schedule and assigns the best five available officials to that game, and they commit to being there unless extenuating circumstances arise. Coaches hate unknowns. While they cannot control the officials' actions on the field, they can, at this level, control which officials are on the field.

That commitment represents our word not only to the coaches, but also to our fellow officials, who don't like change either. Officials assigned to an important game want to know with whom they will be working. They don't like last-minute surprises. It happens, but for the most part, everybody concerned wants to know who is assigned so they can prepare for and point toward that game.

A last-minute change where someone is added to the crew creates a ripple effect. First, an official is suddenly thrust into a situation for which he might not be mentally prepared. Second, that particular official hasn't worked with that specific crew, and each crew has a unique identity. Coaches agree on who will work that game, and that's who they want there, end of conversation. Suddenly, one official forgets that day is his anniversary and needs to take his wife out for dinner instead of working a football game. The chapter secretary now has to find the next best official and move him into that game, which makes for a tough situation all around.

I was really blessed and never missed a game. When I received my schedule, I thought through every possible scenario such as birthdays or anything else that could cause a conflict. Now, have I worked games when I didn't feel great? Absolutely. But I've been blessed with good health. By the end of my fifth year, I received my first playoff assignment and wound up getting five of them that year. It was one of those times that when it happened, it really happened. That gave me a chance to work higher-profile games and work with better crews.

I was told early in my career that working one position and becoming proficient at it would create a better chance of advancing than working several positions. Virtually no one advanced to the college level as a referee. That led me to become a head linesman and take care of the chain. Eventually, I reached a point where that was the only position I wanted to work. I thoroughly understood its mechanics and nuances.

The dream of every high school official is to move up to the next level, whatever the next level might be. A guy working junior varsity games wants to move to the varsity level. Guys working varsity games want to move to the next classification. Once there, they look for opportunities to work at the small-college level. If they are fortunate enough to make it to that level, they're thinking about moving beyond.

I can remember when I first started working Youth Football League games. They played them all around Lubbock, right after church each Sunday. I'd work three games a week with parents sitting around the field in lawn chairs. Players were anywhere from seven to twelve years old, and I never knew what level I would get assigned to. I was just told to be at a certain field at a certain time and work the games of the teams that showed up.

All fans are partisan, but few fans are as partisan as parents and grandparents, which is what we had for the most part at that level. What fans didn't understand about those games is that the officials working the games were young, inexperienced, and did not yet possess a complete knowledge of the rulebook. In other words, they weren't going to be too good. If we were really good officials, we wouldn't be working YFL games on a Sunday afternoon. The guys doing that are just trying to get better.

For their part, most fans who watch football on television equate whatever they see to levels several notches above the YFL. They expect perfection, and officiating is one of the only avocations in which the participants are expected to be perfect today and even better the next time out. At the YFL officiating level, that's just not going to happen.

But that was all part of the process for us. Chapter members accumulated points based on games worked, and we had to accumulate a certain number of points to move from one classification of official to the next. In Texas, we had five classifications, with Division I being the highest. Typically, the official who reaches Division I is more seasoned, a little more well-known, and somewhat more likely to be assigned to a higher classification game.

The expectations are different at every level. I remember my first week of working Thursdays with seventh-grade, eighth-grade, and junior varsity games. There is nothing in the world quite like watching a seventh-grade game, which, for many kids, represents the first time they have put on pads and lined up across from another player who was actually going to hit them.

We aren't going to call holding on those guys. In a seventh-grade game, we would tell players, "No. 17, keep your hands in. I saw you grab him. If you do it again, I will flag you." We talk a lot to kids at that level. We can throw flags all afternoon, but we try to understand the situation and call the game accordingly.

Then it's the eighth-grade game. They've played a year, so they know a little more about what they should be doing. They don't have the same wide-eyed look at the line of scrimmage. Speed picks up; play is a little crisper. After that, the junior varsity trots out. Those are high school kids, bigger and faster. They have a better grasp of the game's intricacies.

In 1989, I worked the Texas–Colorado game, which was a Monday night contest on national television with Bill McCartney coaching Colorado and David McWilliams coaching Texas. It was a big-time game, and I was the line judge.

The next morning I flew back to Lubbock and drove home to Morton. On Thursday of that week, I worked the seventh-grade, eighth-grade, and junior varsity games at Morton High School. We got through the first two games with no problem. The JV game was rolling along, and it was a fairly tight contest. The visiting coach had no idea who I was, and he was on me about not knowing the rules and berating me while he was getting beat.

I'm standing there thinking—egotistically, I admit—I just worked a national TV game Monday night, and I'm out here three days later being told I don't know a thing about football by a JV coach. It was ridiculous. Finally, the guy working the chain asked the coach if he saw the Texas–Colorado game earlier in the week. Of course he had. Then he told him that I worked the game. I didn't hear a word the second half about not knowing the rules. Looking back, I probably should have flagged him. I didn't flag many coaches in my career, but he's one who deserved it.

Early in my career, I could have worked seven games in a typical week between YFL, seventh-grade, eighth-grade, JV, and Friday night varsity games. I did work nine games one weekend—three Thursday, one Friday, two Saturday, and three YFL games Sunday afternoon. It was a lot of work, but I knew I needed it, just as players need practice reps to improve steadily.

Make no mistake, football rules are complicated. There are exceptions to the exceptions. You prepare for that by working your schedule of games, studying, taking tests, accumulating points, and moving up. My goal was to move to Division I and get to work 5A games. When I did reach the Southwest Conference as an official, I was still a Division II official, which was unheard of. I reached Division I pretty quickly after that. Working high school games is a unique experience. It doesn't matter if it's a Class 5A or 1A school; you get excited about where you're going and who you're going to be working with.

I got into the Southwest Conference because of Clint Ramsey. He was a Southwest Conference official and athletic director at South Plains College in Levelland at the time. I worked a few games with him because he was in our chapter, and like me, he loved high school football. Early in my career we worked a Class 5A game at Plainview together for coach Greg Sherwood.

It was a beautiful West Texas night, and the stadium was full. Clint knew it was one of my first experiences working a big 5A game. He looked at me and made a simple declaration. "Now you know why God made Friday night."

I loved high school football and being around the game, and here I was working a big game with a Southwest Conference official on the crew in a perfect environment. It was unforgettable. Clint lived in Levelland at the time, and I lived in Morton, so I would often pick him up when we worked games together. I enjoyed listening to his stories about what he had seen as an official. His was a great influence on me.

Sometime after that, Clint became athletic director at Angelo State in San Angelo, Texas, before coming to Texas Tech as an academic adviser in the athletic department. Becoming a Tech employee meant he could no longer work as an SWC official because Tech was a member of the conference, so Lubbock didn't have an official on the league staff. In those days, coaches wanted each school to be represented, and Lubbock's was gone with Clint's resignation.

Ken Faulkner, the SWC supervisor of officials, called Clint and discussed worthy replacements. Clint recommended me, and for that I will forever be in his debt. He could have mentioned anyone. Ken Faulkner knew me. He'd seen me work, and he knew I was a dedicated official.

I was in a board meeting at our bank when my secretary came in and said I needed to return a call to Ken Faulkner at the Southwest Conference office. I thought, *Sure, somebody is playing a prank on me.*

It was no prank. I was about to become part of the legendary Southwest Conference.

What's the Call?

Team A fumbles the ball backward. In an attempt to recover, team B touches the ball, and it rolls into Team A's end zone, where Team A recovers the ball. What is the ruling?

A. Touchback for Team A.

B. Safety, award Team B two points.

C. Play the next down at the previous spot, Team A's ball.

(See page 196 for answer.)

CHAPTER THREE:
THE SWC AND ME

"Football is only a game. Spiritual things are eternal. Nevertheless,
BEAT TEXAS!"

—Seen on a church sign in Arkansas
the week prior to a Texas game

THE FIRST PERSON to call me after I became a Southwest Conference official was Tim Millis, then a field judge in the league.

"I understand you are one of the new officials on our roster, and I wanted to call and personally welcome you to the Southwest Conference," he said. "We won't be on the same crew, but I hope I get to work with you."

I was still coming to terms with the heady reality that I had even been asked to join the Southwest Conference. I had yet to attend a meeting or go to any scrimmages. Ken Faulkner called and said he needed a line judge. As of this point, that was pretty much the extent of my knowledge.

Of course, I had spent the balance of my career thus far working as a head linesman, so I was looking forward to the challenges a new position would provide. As for Ken, he considered the two positions virtually interchangeable, and to a large extent, he was right. Each position is on the line of scrimmage, although the responsibilities at the snap are somewhat different. Ken told me, "I know you've worked as a head linesman, but I need a line judge."

The position didn't matter all that much to me. I was thrilled just to be a part of the league. This was the summer of 1988, and I would later learn that Tim Millis, who had taken time to welcome me into the league, was on his way to greatness in officiating circles. He would become one of the most respected NFL officials around, working three NFC championship games as well as two Super Bowls. After building that resume, he went on to become supervisor of officials in the newly born Big 12 in 1996, which means he would eventually become my boss. Again, this was no coincidence.

That was later, though. For now, I was zeroed in on the SWC, one of the most storied leagues in college football history. We're talking about a conference that produced such great players as Sammy Baugh, John David Crow, Doak Walker, Earl Campbell, and Andre Ware. Legends' shadows were cast everywhere.

I had been working for a number of years at Texas Tech summer practices to help keep myself sharp for the small-college games that I would work, and as the summer of 1988 unfolded I was spending a lot of time working those practices in Lubbock. I was watching snaps and pass drills and trying to see as much full-speed college football as possible. One week, Ken Faulkner, the league's supervisor of officials, called and said he was sending a crew to work an intrasquad scrimmage at Texas A&M. Ken thought it would be a great time for me to get in a little work. The line judge on that particular crew couldn't make it, so it was an opportunity to see a team besides Tech and spend time with a seasoned crew.

Loyd Dale was the referee on that crew, and James Wilson was the head linesman. Joe Darden was the umpire, Mike Wetzel was the side judge, Ron Murphy was the back judge, and Tim Millis was the field judge. That was my first taste of working with a full-fledged Southwest Conference crew, and the fact that it was at Texas A&M was a big thrill. I'd never been to Kyle Field.

A&M's coach, Jackie Sherrill, organized the scrimmage, and he wanted game-like conditions throughout, including a full officiating crew. I flew to Dallas and drove to College Station with the crew. On the way back after the scrimmage, every single one of those guys spent time giving me pointers and advice. I received another call from the supervisor the next week. He said Rice was having a scrimmage, and he wanted me to go to Houston and work.

"I went with those guys last week," I said.

"I know that, and they said you need a lot of work," Ken replied.

Right away, I knew I had not impressed the most experienced crew in the Southwest Conference. I was a rookie official who still had not seen his first live SWC snap. I was pretty sure I was being sent to Rice because that crew had told the supervisor I wasn't very good, which was surprising to me.

I went to Rice, and the regular line judge was there with the crew this time, so we took turns working. That line judge was hard to forget; his name was Roger Rogers and he was from Rogers, Arkansas. Rogers was a good official. He had a way about him. His mechanics were not that solid, but he had great judgment.

We were never on the same crew because we worked the same position. Coaches liked Rogers because he had a slow Arkansas drawl and was the kind of guy who could disarm a volatile coach with his demeanor and the way he talked. I learned a lot from him.

My first regular season assignment was a Rice–Southwestern Louisiana game in Lafayette, Louisiana. This game wasn't going to be televised—period—so if I messed up, the entire world wouldn't have to know. I was working with a great crew that was split between the SWC and the Sun Belt Conference. Not only was it my first game, but it was also the first game for the referee on that crew. As it turned out, it wasn't much of a game. The season was a few weeks old, and of course, the more experienced members of our crew knew the two new guys were unsure of themselves, nervous and a little bit scared.

So those older guys were going to have some fun with us.

The game was moving along all right, and I saw an offsides by the defense and threw my flag. The head linesman, Dickey Taylor, also threw his flag and blew his whistle, killing the play. Once the play is blown dead, mechanics call for the head linesman, line judge, and umpire to get together, sort everything out and agree on the infraction. Then the referee enters the picture, asks what the call is, and takes it from there. I go running in there after throwing my first flag. The head linesman is from the other conference.

"What do you have?" he asked.

"I've got contact by the defense," I explain.

"You do? Didn't you see the ball moving?" he asked with a straight face.

I was stunned, and he immediately died laughing. I'm sure he was waiting for me to throw my first flag and be certain about the call. When he asked that question, my eyes got as big as silver dollars. Of course, the ball had not moved. He was just yanking my chain.

We had a lot of flags that day, which was the crew's way of picking on that rookie referee. They called everything that could possibly be called; it was an inordinate number of penalties, but they wanted to make sure the referee had a memorable night.

Officials had a number of traditions in the Southwest Conference, and one of those occurred after you worked your first game. One of the other crew members carried the ball off the field, let the air out and gave it to the rookie. Rest assured, officials "securing" game balls is a practice not sanctioned by the participating schools or the conferences, but it goes on, and most of the time nothing is said. If you asked for one, it would probably be given to you, but what fun would that be?

Jim Evans was the back judge that day, and he gave me a heads-up during the game.

"When this game is over, we're going to get you a ball as a memento for your first game," he said.

"How does that work?" I asked innocently.

"Don't worry about it; we'll handle it."

As it turned out, Evans took a game ball. Later, we all met at the hotel to write our game reports, and as we were sitting around, they presented me and the referee with game balls that these veteran officials had "secured."

"You will need to let the air out of it and put it in your bag because the schools really don't like this happening," one of them told me.

I was all right with that because I was glad to have the ball. About that time, Evans went down the hall, got on a phone and called the room. He pretended to be an official from Southwestern Louisiana who said he saw the line judge carrying off the ball after the game and wanted it brought back. I thought I was in trouble. Rookie officials fall for those kinds of pranks.

Pulling practical jokes on each other is a time-honored tradition among officials, as I would learn. I remember making an incorrect call in the last game Grant Teaff ever coached at Baylor. The call became one of those ESPN highlights that takes on a life of its own, and sometime around the middle of the week, I got a call at the bank from a *Sports Illustrated* writer who wanted to talk about it.

I'd already had a pretty bad week. I made a bad call, ended up on ESPN, and now I had a national media representative on the line. What do I do? I took the call, even though officials are discouraged from talking to the media. I made a poor decision.

It was Evans on the line, and the first words out of his mouth were, "You shouldn't have taken the call." He was always pulling those kinds of pranks. It was not unheard of for officials, in the depths of their depression over a blown call, to receive a call like that from a fellow official. It came with being part of the brotherhood and could bring a smile to your face when you needed one most.

My second game in the SWC was Texas A&M against Northwestern Louisiana. Do you see a pattern here? I obviously wasn't working headliner games. Jackie Sherrill was A&M's coach. Our umpire, Bill Voss, called him "Coach Jackie," and he let Sherrill know right away that a rookie was working his sideline. Needless to say, Northwestern Louisiana wasn't much of a challenge for the Aggies that day, so Coach Jackie spent a good part of his day indoctrinating me into the SWC.

I will never forget one play when I called A&M for holding, wiping out a fairly good play for the Aggies. The fans were booing, and I was thinking anyone could have seen that one. Sherrill was about thirty yards down the field from me, but he turned around and sprinted down the sideline toward me. The A&M fans saw this and roared.

He got in my face, shook his finger at me, and said, "That was a good call. I saw that."

The fans didn't know what he said, but they assumed he was chewing on me, which caused the volume inside the stadium to reach a new level. Jackie and Bill Voss are old acquaintances, and they loved it. The other officials loved it, too, because they thought Coach Jackie had just ripped this poor rookie official.

Voss and Jackie Sherrill had one of those love-hate relationships. I was on that crew with Bill for five years. Voss had a philosophy that he would call holding once in the first half and once in the second half, whether it was needed or not. We once worked a game between A&M and Baylor in which Bill called A&M for holding twice in a short span of time.

Sherrill walked over to me and said, "You tell Voss if he calls holding on us one more time, I'm going to whip his butt."

After the next play, I told Bill exactly what Sherrill said. He stopped the clock and walked over to Sherrill to ask him about it.

"Coach Jackie, I hear you're gonna whip my butt if I call holding on you again," Voss said.

"That's right, Voss!" Coach Sherrill responded.

"You know," Voss said. "I think we could sell tickets to that."

I was standing there with my mouth wide open because I couldn't believe he stopped the clock to pick an argument with Jackie Sherrill. If you were going to pick a fight with a coach, I figured, there'd be better opportunities to do it than that. Meanwhile, the two of them parted, both laughing.

I don't have the persona for cutting up with coaches. I had a give-and-take relationship like that with Oklahoma's Bob Stoops, but I was in a different mindset on the sideline. I tried not to pick conversations many times, but I did on occasion. I was always in awe of officials who could pull that kind of stuff and get away with it. Some of the old-time officials, guys like Frank Shepherd, were like that. Shepherd, an SWC referee from Midland, Texas, is a good friend of mine who worked for the Big 12 observing officiating crews after he retired from the field.

Frank had a knack for being funny at the most unusual times. He was once working a Texas–Arkansas game in Little Rock back in the 1980s. It was a tight game, and Arkansas fumbled the ball late. The players were digging around, and the officials got in there to find that Texas had recovered. Frank pointed the Longhorns' way and said, "Our ball!" Talk about a stunned crowd. Frank had a reason, though. Legendary Arkansas sports writer Orville Henry always castigated

Texas officials, and a story in the *Arkansas Gazette* that day talked about the crew being loaded with Texas officials.

Nothing makes an official angrier than to be accused of being biased. We're not. It's not part of our deal. We don't care if Texas wins or Arkansas wins. Frank was just slamming a sports writer when he said that. He could care less who won the game.

Here's another story about Frank. He was working a Texas–Baylor game one year when David McWilliams was the Longhorns' coach. It was Baylor's homecoming. Part of the officials' pregame routine is that the referee and umpire go see the head coaches seventy-five minutes before kickoff to learn whether any trick plays might be used. They saw the Baylor coach, and then they walked across the field to the Texas dressing room. Nothing big happens at those meetings. On the way to see McWilliams, Frank got one green balloon and one gold balloon and tied them to his belt.

He said to McWilliams, "Coach, it's our homecoming today. Do you have any trick plays?"

The Texas coaches thought it was hilarious. If I had tried that, I'd have been expelled from the conference. Those starched-and-pressed officials out there would cringe at even hearing that. Frank wanted people to relax, though. It was his way of relieving tension in a high-stress environment.

* * *

The only other game I worked during the 1988 season was a league matchup between Texas Tech and Rice. That was my baptism into Division I officiating, and all it did was whet my appetite to play a larger role in 1989. I thought I had learned a lot coming into my second year. I looked forward to our summer clinics each year. I always had to pinch myself to realize how privileged and blessed I was to be sitting in that room with that select group of men who had a huge responsibility, which was to call every Southwest Conference game that year. I would look around the room and think about those guys and reflect on the fact that we had an awesome responsibility to go out into the middle of those heated battles, because the league had a lot of intense rivalries.

Texas A&M–Texas, Texas A&M–Texas Tech, TCU–SMU, Houston–Rice, Texas A&M–Baylor. Those were heated confrontations, and it didn't matter if one team hadn't won a game all year. When that rival rolled into town, it was expected to go down to the wire. I would sit there and think about that and know that the guys in that room were looking forward to that challenge.

Let me assure you that officials understand all the nuances of the game. If it's a big play in a big game, the officials aren't surprised. They know fourth-and-one late in the game. They know the scenarios. I wanted the big play to come my way because I wanted to make the call. I've known some officials over the years who hoped the big play would go the other way. With guys at the SWC level, however, you could almost see them throw their shoulders back when the teams came to the line of scrimmage. They were ready for that play and wanted it to land at their feet.

The old Southwest Conference might have been the last of the fun college officiating environments. There never was a conference like that where all the schools were in the same state, except Arkansas, and it wasn't that far from Texas to Fayetteville or Little Rock. Supervisor of officials Ken Faulkner was a former league official. As far as Ken was concerned, someone either could or couldn't officiate. He didn't put pressure on anyone when they had a bad week because he knew they were aware of it and would do everything possible to improve their performance the next week. He was an unbelievable guy to work for, with such a great sense about officials. I can't tell anything about an official's ability until I step on the field and work with him, but Ken had unusual insight. He could stand on the sideline or watch from the press box and be able to tell if an official had what it took to stand up to the pressures of officiating college football.

Officiating is physically demanding to an extent, but it is even more mentally demanding. You must be at your best every play. Each snap requires a period of intense concentration. You have one level of concentration while a play is going on and a different one between plays.

The league was fun for other reasons, as well. We had a number of old-time officials who were seasoned in that league and became college football officials in an age different from the ones there today. They were different people from a different era of football. Those guys were in their forties and fifties and many of them had played in the 1940s and '50s. They understood it was a game but possessed a different outlook. The game might seem like life or death this week, but they still had another game to officiate next week.

They also understood that football is a game played by humans, coached by humans, and officiated by humans, so human error is part of the game. Once you realize that, you understand that is what makes the game what it is. Officials make mistakes. Coaches make mistakes. Players make mistakes. Obviously, I can't speak for all officials, but not one among the officials I worked with favored instant replay. I, too, am no fan of instant replay; it is an attempt to take the human element out of the game.

The first time I walked into the middle of a Texas A&M–Texas game, Thanksgiving Day 1991, was phenomenal. It was a blessing to be part of the aura and history of the SWC. Unfortunately, the whole persona of the league changed the minute Arkansas started talking about leaving. There wasn't any talk about the Big 12 at first, but there was plenty of talk about change. People knew the league didn't have the power to draw the kind of television exposure necessary for long-term survival. Transitions were taking place elsewhere, too. Faulkner retired, and Wendell Shelton took over as supervisor of officials.

Wendell knew the conference wasn't going to last, and he knew officiating was changing. Ken was kind of the last of a breed of supervisors who'd pick a guy and stick with him. If the official made a mistake, Ken knew it was hard on him and would offer a chance at redemption. Wendell, on the other hand, knew college football was becoming a big business.

An official who had been in the league a long time and didn't continue to make colossal mistakes in games was going to be all right. If an old crew had been together for a while, it could survive making mistakes. Wendell knew things were changing, and he tried to bring more input to officiating than we had received from Ken. It can be argued both ways whether that was the thing to do, but change was inevitable.

A certain amount of professional jealousy existed among the referees of the six SWC crews. Egos were involved, and referees wanted their crew to get the best games. Wendell had been successful as an SWC referee because he had some pretty good officials on his crew. When he became supervisor and had to start making assignments, he was not as universally loved as his predecessor. Wendell had a tough job, and the SWC didn't have the same reputation in 1994 that it had a mere five years earlier. It was still seen as a quality football league, but it wasn't the same without Arkansas. Many veteran officials retired, and Wendell brought in some who were not of the same caliber as the guys who left.

I think we were struggling with the level of officiating at the same time that the conference was struggling with its own identity during its final years. When I came into the league, I couldn't see the problems. I was just glad to be there. It was fun, but by the early to mid-1990s, I could see dramatic changes in the league and not just in the caliber of officials. The SWC seemed to lose some real credibility. You could just see it. From the competition to the TV coverage, the perception throughout college football was that the SWC was dying. And it was. Because of that, it just wasn't as much fun as it had been in years past.

The league still had big games, though. Texas A&M against Texas was a big game. The Texas–Oklahoma game was a major event. Those great Saturday afternoon rivalries were still a big deal. If we officiated the Texas–Baylor game, it was sold out, but when we worked the Houston–Baylor game, the stadium wouldn't be full. An official could tell it wasn't the same atmosphere. I say all that now with the experience of having worked Big 12 games for ten years. With the exception of Kansas, the stadiums in the new league were pretty full. Kansas struggled early, but thanks to the tremendous recent success the program has enjoyed under coach Mark Mangino, that has changed. To me and many others, the SWC was pretty close to being a ghost of itself even before it was officially over.

And it was an example of how things changed down the stretch. The last SWC game I worked was Texas at Texas Christian. Jim Evans was our back judge, and he pulled up lame on the first punt of the game. He came over to the sideline, and we had a conference official there who was recording infractions but wasn't in uniform. He hadn't worked many games at that time but is now in the NFL. We worked a six-man crew the rest of the first half. During halftime, the guy keeping the fouls who was in his street clothes put on Evans's uniform and worked his position during the second half.

The funny thing about it is Evans was much larger than this guy, so the hat was over his ears and his pants were way too big. He looked like a junior high kid who had crashed the crew because his clothes were so baggy. That would have never happened in the Big 12, but it was stuff we could get away with in the SWC.

The league ceased operation in 1995, but my final two seasons with the SWC were absolute torture for me because Shelton assigned me to the worst crew I have ever been associated with. The 1994 and '95 seasons were not a lot of fun. I'm not pointing fingers at anyone; we just never meshed as a crew. We didn't grade out well. I was awarded a bowl game in 1994, and when that season ended, Wendell asked me how I felt about that crew.

"We had a tough year," was the way I sized it up.

"You guys weren't very good," he said. "How would you feel about moving to another crew?"

I told him I wanted to stay where I was. I made a mistake and thought I could singlehandedly bring that crew together. It was the worst decision I ever made in my officiating career. I'd worked with those guys and liked them personally, but as a crew, we didn't click. I knew I was one of the better officials in the league and felt like the crew looked to me for leadership. That crew didn't mesh well in 1994. I could have moved, but I felt like I could help make the crew better, so I stayed on for 1995. It was the worst season of my life.

There were some good guys on the crew, though. Mike Wetzel was part of that group, and he probably influenced my decision to stay. We were friends who had worked the 1993 national championship together. Jim Evans was the back judge. Professionally, we did not mesh—we had different philosophies about what needed to be called and what didn't. Personally, I liked him a lot. The head linesman and field judge were simply in over their heads. We had a referee with a personality problem and an umpire who I thought was in the twilight zone most of the time. This umpire would get in a game and not be able to talk because he was either so enthralled with the game or he was half scared. I never could figure out which. He just couldn't utter a word during a game.

I say all of that as a preface to the Texas Tech–Baylor game that year. Tech was pretty good, and all of the problems within our crew culminated that Saturday afternoon in Waco. We got into a heated, tight situation and didn't handle it well. One series of plays demonstrated what happens when a struggling crew is pushed to the brink.

Tech had the ball first-and-goal inside the Baylor five. The Red Raiders were the better team athletically and in all facets of the game, but they had not played that well and Baylor was ahead. Despite that, Tech was still in position to win. A few plays later, and it's fourth down at the one. The Tech quarterback handed the ball off. I was on Tech's right side, and the Raiders went over left tackle. A big pile-up occurred at the line of scrimmage, and I couldn't see anything. It was the head linesman's call. Next thing we knew, everyone was stacked up at the line of scrimmage, and the ball was rolling around in the end zone. I came in. The head linesman came in. The play was over and Baylor had the ball in the end zone. Touchdown? Fumble? We closed down on the play. I looked at the head linesman, and he shrugged his shoulders. He froze and could not make the call. Something has to be called. The clock is running, and the referee has not stopped it.

We finally stopped the clock, but more than twenty seconds had run off. We asked the head linesman whether it was a touchdown or a fumble, but he couldn't call it either. The first thing we had to do was get the clock corrected, but the referee would not put any time back on the clock. Tech head coach Spike Dykes was screaming. The head linesman couldn't make the call. We didn't put time back on the clock, and Tech didn't score in a 9–7 loss, one of only three defeats for the Red Raiders that season. Since then, we've looked at the play dozens of times, and the replays are all inconclusive. Like any call, officials have to make a decision, and we don't have the luxury of being able to wait.

That situation was building within this crew for two years, and it boiled down to a time when the crew had to come together and make a correct call, and we couldn't do it. I have never been so disgusted with officiating as I was at the end of that game and that season. As it turned out, that was the season the conference folded, and the league made its decision about which officials would transition into the Big 12. I almost didn't make it because of the two years I spent on that crew.

I learned the hard way that no one official can make a crew better. I was naïve and confident in my ability that I could make a difference, but it never happened. It was the low point in my career as a Division I official. I felt like a failure, and all of our shortcomings showed up in the waning moments of one game.

Weaknesses can sometimes be camouflaged in a crew, but eventually, if a guy doesn't belong at that level, it turns into a situation where the character of the crew and the individual officials are revealed. We either float together or sink together. Not surprisingly, I didn't get a bowl game at the end of the '95 season, which was disappointing to me because I was becoming accustomed to going each year. I felt individually that I had done things correctly, but I sank as part of a crew that was a collective failure.

Change was coming, though. The Big 12 had emerged and included four former members of the Southwest Conference. Tim Millis, the man who had welcomed me to the Southwest Conference almost ten years earlier, had been named supervisor of officials for the new league. Tim knew I could officiate, but being on a bad crew for the past two years was working against me.

It was a down moment for me. I had spent a lot of time studying the rulebook and not enough time studying the Bible. I had spent a lot of time building my officiating career instead of building my spiritual relationship with Jesus. Now, at a time when someone in this position could call upon his faith, I couldn't make the call.

The Southwest Conference was going away, and I had no idea if I was going anywhere.

What's the Call?

On a legal forward pass beyond the neutral zone, Team A (Player No. 80) and Team B (Player No. 60) attempt to catch a pass thrown in the area of No. 80. Team A (Player No. 14), who is not attempting to catch the pass, blocks Team B (Player No. 65) downfield while the pass is in the air. What is the ruling?

A. Ignore the contact, no foul.

B. Foul by No. 14, but ignore it because it is away from the play.

C. Offensive pass interference, penalize Team A fifteen yards from previous spot.

(See page 196 for answer.)

CHAPTER FOUR:
IN THE ROOM

"You can learn more character on the two-yard line than anywhere else in life."

— Paul Dietzel, former head coach, Louisiana State University

" CALL IT WHILE IT'S IN THE AAAAIIIIRRR ! "

BEING IN A roomful of college football officials might not seem like such a great experience—unless, of course, you happen to be an official enjoying that experience for the first time. To me, that was part of the mystique of joining the Southwest Conference officiating fraternity. It was a fairly exclusive club, and it took years of effort before I became a member.

My first experience along these lines came in July 1988, when I attended the Southwest Conference football officials' annual summer meeting in Houston. We had three new officials entering the league that year: Jon Bible, Rogers Redding, and myself, and beforehand, some of the more seasoned officials gave us a heads-up on how the meeting worked.

"Rookies don't talk in this meeting, so keep your mouth shut and listen," one of them said. "If you have a question, ask one of us later. I wouldn't ask it in that room."

Naturally, within the first hour of the first meeting, Jon Bible was standing up asking questions. At that time, Jon was already an outstanding, established baseball umpire in the Southwest Conference, and President Ronald Reagan had named him to be chairman of a committee on national baseball rules, so Jon was unlikely to hold his tongue. That's one of the many things I like about him. He doesn't back down from anybody. It was interesting to watch. At the time, I didn't know Jon, but I had heard of him. He is truly an outspoken individual.

One of the first things that get discussed in these meetings are rules changes. The hardest rule to enforce is the one that has been recently changed because we might not have encountered it much on the field. By the new season, if we had not seen the infraction, it was difficult for us to administer because we spent the bulk of our time going over new rule changes for the current season.

We watched numerous films, and we always had an emphasis on rules involving sportsmanship. The NCAA emphasizes sportsmanship each year, and many rule changes in recent years have reflected that emphasis. One year, the rule about taking your helmet off on the field was changed. Orchestrated celebrations are an infraction. Sportsmanship issues consume a lot of time in our meetings. My take on this whole issue is that officials are an easy group for the NCAA, conferences, and schools to hold responsible for matters they should address themselves.

Take, for example, the dress code for players. That is addressed specifically in the rule book. Dress code issues such as socks being the same distance up or down the calf of the leg and the same color on all players of the same team sounds easy to accomplish. Well, it isn't. These days, players all want to be different. As officials, we think those issues should be addressed in the locker room by team personnel rather than making the officials the sock police.

Something else we spend time watching at the summer meetings are films illustrating specific infractions. We will spend hours watching replay after replay of pass interference, holding, and neutral zone infractions such as false starts and offsides. After that, we break out into position groups. For instance, all referees go to one room. All side judges go to another room. The line judges go to another. You get the picture.

Those breakout meetings are led by the more senior people manning those positions, and they are specifically designed for rookies such as me. I went into my first position meeting with six other line judges. At that time in the Southwest Conference, we had fifty-two officials. That breaks down to seven full seven-man crews and three who would serve as "swing" guys, filling in on an as-needed basis.

My first line judge meeting included some great guys, such as Walt Coleman. At that time, Coleman was an outstanding line judge and is now a superior NFL referee, having worked a number of important games. It was Coleman's departure for the NFL after the 1988 season which made room for me to become a full-time SWC line judge on a regular crew. Of the seven line judges in that room that day, three were from Arkansas. In addition to Walt, Roger Rogers, and Ron Underwood also were from Arkansas and each had established reputations as officials of quality.

I was impressed just listening to those guys talk about mechanics. No matter how good one's judgment is, mechanics are critical. If an official is in the wrong spot at the wrong time and makes a call—even if it is the correct call—the first thing he is going to hear is that he was out of position and was lucky—if he got the call right. More times than not, an official in the wrong spot will make a questionable call.

The official might be one step too deep in the backfield to have made a certain call or he might have needed to be more outside the sideline to have a clear view of the play. Sometimes fans might see a head linesman or line judge running to get out of the way when a play is in progress. It's hard to officiate when you're running for your life.

As an aside, officials working the wing positions, such as line judges, start on the sideline and preferably are a step off so the sideline is clearly in front of them. With twenty-two players on the field and fifty or sixty more right behind them, they don't have a lot of room, but they have to be outside the sideline so they can have a clear view of the play should it come their way.

Much of that is learning the mechanics of who an official's key is when the ball is snapped. That represented a real learning curve for me. We keyed on players in high school games, but at that level we were pretty much playing zone, so we were watching areas of the field, rather than specific players.

In a college game with a seven-man crew, five officials watch five eligible receivers on each play. The trick is each official knowing which receiver he has so two sets of eyes are not on one receiver while another receiver is running loose with no one watching him. With multiple sets, shifts, and men in motion, an official might be keyed on one receiver when a team first comes to the line of scrimmage and then, when the ball is snapped, change his key several times depending on everything that has happened in the time leading up to the snap.

That is why the crew concept is so important. The mechanics of crew officiating vary from conference to conference and even from crew to crew in spite of what the official *Seven Man Mechanics* book produced by the NCAA says. That is important for new officials to understand. I worked three games with three different crews my first year in the conference, and it seemed to be a pretty subjective process, but I came to learn that each crew had its own nuances regarding the way the mechanics of certain situations were handled. Thus, the importance of a good pregame conference.

The first year an official steps on a field with a college crew, he can't be expected to know little things like that. It doesn't matter how good that official is, if he is not watching the right spot at the right time, he will miss the call. Understanding those little things comes from sitting in meetings week after week, year after year, watching film, and communicating with one's crew about what's going to happen when.

Something else those veteran officials gave us in our first summer meeting were insights into the personalities of specific coaches. They would say, "Jackie Sherrill is going to be on you all the time regardless of the calls you make, so get ready. Now Grant Teaff never says a word, but if you get something wrong, he will be down your collar. And Jack Pardee is pretty easygoing. He won't say anything one way or another."

Armed with this information we had an idea going into certain games whether it was going to be a tough week or not, and we had to prepare for that mentally. I loved to work in front of coaches like Nebraska's Tom Osborne because I knew that unless I completely blew a call, they wouldn't say much to me. They spent their time coaching, and they knew everything would balance out over the course of the season. I also knew that other coaches were going to ride the officials because that's what they do.

Some coaches are really tolerant of officials, and my impression was always that we were tolerant of the coaches who were tolerant of us. That's human nature. Some coaches are going to continually criticize an official about calling or not calling something that isn't going to make a difference in the outcome of the game. Thinking about that from the viewpoint of the young official I was two decades ago, my preference is that the coaches leave me alone and I will do a better job.

If a coach is continually harassing an official, it doesn't matter how good that official is, it will pull away some part of his focus. That stuff should be water rolling off his back, but it does take away some percentage of his concentration. Of course, I always try to remember one of the oldest officiating adages: If you make a mistake and know you made a mistake, you have to put it completely out of your mind and focus on the next play.

When an official doesn't do that, he will make another mistake, and that ball will keep rolling. That is a difficult concept for a young official to learn. The time to deal with a mistake is after the game. Forget it during the game.

I've seen officials and crews who have been suspended for making a bad call. That possibility has always been there, but it seems to be a bigger threat today than it was twenty years ago. From being in the room, I can say that when an official or a crew is suspended, it's rarely a result of making just one mistake. That crew or that official has more often than not made some mistakes already, and the supervisor has had a conversation about it. Generally, it's a result of prior mistakes or downgrades in their game films, little problems taken together that by themselves aren't big enough to result in that kind of discipline. But those little things add up, and then the big play comes along. That's when people are set down. Fortunately, I've never been on a crew that had that happen to them. I've been hit on a "ding" tape after a game, just like everyone else in my profession has, but this unpleasant experience doesn't carry the sting of a suspension.

Now, you're probably wondering what the heck a "ding" tape is. Hang on. We'll get there, but a bit of history first. In the old Southwest Conference days, officials would work a game and probably have a few plays in there that they thought they called right, but wanted to be sure they did. At that time, we received no feedback from the conference on our performance, and I didn't have a problem with that my first year.

Ken Faulkner never said anything much until the end of the year, when we received our rankings. At the end of that 1988 season, I was the No. 2–rated line judge in the conference, but I worked only three games. I knew I didn't have much opportunity to mess things up in that first year.

I worked a full season the next year and finished No. 3. I was feeling pretty good and thought I'd be in line to get a bowl assignment, but the veteran guys said guys who had not been around very long didn't go to bowl games. And they were right. The same was true in 1990. Finally, in 1991, I graded out well enough to receive an assignment to work the Aloha Bowl. Not only was it my first bowl and in Hawaii, but it also had two great teams—Stanford and Georgia Tech. Stanford was coached by Dennis Green and a young assistant by the name of Tyrone Willingham, whom I had gotten to know when he was an assistant on the staff at Rice. Georgia Tech was coached by Bobby Ross. As it turned out, that was the final college game for each of those head coaches. Both went to the NFL, with Ross moving to the San Diego Chargers and Green taking over the Minnesota Vikings. Ross eventually returned to the college game and coached at Army.

I was fortunate enough to go to the Sugar Bowl and the Holiday Bowl the next two years, as well. You've already read about the Sugar Bowl, and the Holiday Bowl was a great experience as well, featuring Brigham Young and Ohio State. Talk about a couple of coaching legends: Ohio State's John Cooper and BYU's LaVell Edwards. It was the first of my three career encounters with Cooper. I saw him at a future Sugar Bowl and worked his sideline in Columbus, Ohio, in a game against Missouri.

Much of that, though, was still a long ways off. After working a couple of games my second year, I called Ken Faulkner.

"Ken, we just had a game where we had a couple of calls that I wanted to know if we got them right, just for my own edification," I said.

"You did just fine," he said. "Keep cutting wood."

That was Ken's philosophy. He supported officials in everything they did unless one displayed a pattern of incompetence.

Wendell Shelton was our referee on that crew, which, besides me, had several young guys. I approached him about it.

"Wendell, we're not getting feedback on how we're doing," I said.

"Be comfortable where you are because you might get some feedback you won't enjoy," he told me.

Ken's philosophy was if an official was on his staff, he could officiate. Otherwise, he was out. That line of thinking began to change in 1992 when Wendell became the league's supervisor of officials. He began providing feedback through game videotapes. At this time, the tapes didn't have audio. We would look at the tape as a crew and receive a sheet with his comments, which might be something like, "Line judge, what were you looking at on this play? Were you in too much of a hurry?" Sure, it was subjective, but it still wasn't the intense process we would later experience under Tim Millis in the Big 12.

I had worked some great games and been a part of some great crews in the Southwest Conference. Then, a smaller group of us made the transition to the Big 12, and one thing we noticed early on was Tim using old SWC game tapes as teaching tools of what not to do as a college football official. The difference between what he wanted and what he expected from us and what we had been producing in the Southwest Conference was night and day. My line judge mechanics in the Big 12 changed overnight. The expectations placed upon us increased astronomically. The training in the summer meeting of 1996 was a very long, very intense experience.

One way Tim addressed improving our officiating mechanics was through the use of NFL training tapes, which focused our attention on what to do on the field. The NFL has a great system for its officials, and Tim brought in some of those officials to help with our training that summer. I worked with an NFL line judge. Tim had an NFL umpire lead the umpire meetings. They gave us specific thoughts from the viewpoint of an experienced NFL official about how to work a position. This is where I met one of my officiating heroes, Red Cashion. Red and I left our hotel to drive out to Valley Ranch, home of the Dallas Cowboys, to do our agility work. I was riding in his car when he gave me one of the most important gems of officiating advice I would ever receive. "When the ball is snapped and you move from your position, know where you are going," he said. The NFL influence on how to officiate in the Big 12 was pronounced. That became even more specific when we began on-the-field training.

The Big 12 had agility drills for each position to see if we were capable physically, and we spent numerous hours in the classroom watching tapes and learning from some of the best officials in the business. The mechanics of the line judge and the head linesman were so orchestrated that you had to take so many steps one way or the other, depending on the situation. It was like relearning the position. Having experience helped, but the league's expectations in every area were more specific than anything I'd encountered previously.

When it came to our reports, the Big 12 didn't want their officials to just write up a holding call by identifying who the penalty was called against. Instead, their expectation was that if a player was called for holding, the report included a verb. Was the player grabbing, hooking, grasping? Likewise, we couldn't simply write that someone was called for pass interference. Did that player hook the receiver? Did he hit the receiver before the ball arrived? We had to specifically describe what we saw.

That specificity enhanced the feedback process because when the Big 12 office graded the game film, they looked at each play and looked at what we described. If we called pass interference and indicated that the cornerback had the receiver in an arm bar, but they didn't see it on the tape, we had a problem. It was an intense grading system for us that first year in the Big 12 and it was scrutiny unlike anything we'd seen before.

The result was that we got better almost overnight. On the downside, a number of guys didn't make it that first year in the Big 12. Some were from the Big Eight and some were from the Southwest Conference, and by surviving prior to arriving in the Big 12, it's reasonable to conclude that they were good at what they had been doing. Some of them simply could not adapt to such increased scrutiny so quickly.

I remember one referee in particular. He stayed only one year, and not because he was fired. He just knew he was not wired to handle that situation. However, because of his great rules knowledge, he became one of Tim's right-hand grading guys, and he was great at that. He just chose not to contribute on the field. I don't think he wanted to live under that particular microscope.

I was fortunate that first year of Big 12 play because Mark Hittner, the head linesman working across from me, was an outstanding official, and I loved working the line of scrimmage with him. The field judge (who works downfield on my sideline) on my crew was Phil Laurie, and Richard Whittenburg was my umpire. Together, those three are as good as any officials I ever worked with my entire career, and that made me improve my game. I knew what the expectations were and was determined to exceed them. Mark Hittner went to the NFL after that first year, and has since worked three Super Bowls. Getting a chance to work with him was a career highlight for me because he is such a great official.

Conversely, the side judge on our crew, who worked down the field from Mark, didn't make it through that first season. Unfortunately, he lacked the courage to throw the penalty flag. By the time we were assigned to the Texas Tech–Texas game about midway through the season, he still hadn't thrown a single flag. Mark was throwing flags for both of them on that side of the field.

Our crew had done a pretty good job that season, but the impact of his reluctance to throw a flag was increasing week by week. Sure enough, in Lubbock that day, Mark made a pass interference call right in front of the side judge a good distance down the field. It was an obvious call, and the side judge should have thrown his flag, but Mark knew there was a good possibility he wouldn't. In the end, it was a clear illustration of an official not surviving the intense scrutiny of this new league.

The conference office continued to refine the system, and in no time it was among the best and most thorough in the country. If a football game generates anything, it's a lot of film. You have television tape as well as two or three tapes from the schools, including film from the end zone and the press box. Most teams have one camera that films just the offense and one that films just the defense. If the game isn't televised, that's at least four tapes. Then you have sideline and end zone views that show everything, and every camera has a different angle.

After the weekend's games were over, the tapes arrived at the conference office, where Tim and his assistants worked Monday and Tuesday grading them. In non-conference weeks, you could have ten to twelve games. Our crews weren't working every game, depending on which teams were at home and which were on the road, but you could have up to seven crews working and seven tapes to grade.

Tim's staff not only looked at every play, but they looked at every play several times. They wanted to see what the line judge was doing on a specific play, what the field judge was doing, the referee, all seven officials. Those grading the tapes were usually NFL officials or retired officials, so they were subjectively grading officials in positions other than the ones they worked themselves, for the most part. In other words, the grader might know something about the mechanics of being an umpire, but he had never walked in the shoes of a line judge. Grading is always subjective, even at its very best.

Consequently, if the grader happened to be a line judge, it was the line judge's week on the hot seat. If it's an umpire grading, he might not know all the nuances of working as a line judge, so he might not notice if the line judge was out of position on a certain play. That can be good or bad. The grader could think that official should have or shouldn't have called something; either way, it's most likely someone without the same perspective.

I always tried to remember that graders are what they are: officials who are not necessarily proficient in every position. This, too, can be good or bad, depending on the situation. However, it was, in my mind, a fair way to judge. The graders looked at every play, and they looked at it at least seven times. If a call was made, the grader provided one of four responses: correct no call, correct call, incorrect call, or incorrect no call. Beyond that, the grader might agree with the official on the call, but say it was a marginal correct call.

For instance, if the umpire called holding, and the grader agreed with what was called and why it was called, he still might maintain that the call could have not been made. Despite that, the grader supported the call. The opposite is when the grader thinks the official should have passed on a call and chooses not to support it. Even though technically the call was correct, it was not popular in the league office because the call did not meet their expectations.

All that scrutiny and feedback led to the creation of what came to be known as the "ding" tape, which showed the good and bad in every crew that week. It was fair. If a great call was made, they would make sure they said so-and-so official made a big-time call and this is what the league was looking for.

The graders turned in their written report from the game tapes. They might say, "The line judge made a great holding call here." Or, "The line judge called holding here. We don't see it. What were you looking at? We're going to downgrade (ding) you here. If you disagree, look at it and send it in. We'll take another look."

I don't think any of us believed that. The conference had already made up its mind. The crew would then receive this tape. It was sent to the referee, who would bring the tape to the game site. Watching the tape was part of our Friday night pregame responsibilities to see what we did right and wrong the week before. I do not know of anything I have dreaded more than each week's Friday night tape session.

Typically, we could walk off that field thinking we had done a pretty good job and then receive the "ding" tape and see we missed holding three times. We got down on ourselves because not only were we seeing this, but the rest of our crew was seeing it, too. Mentally, some guys could not handle that; it would just drive them into the ground. We could get a "ding" for poor work or an "attaboy" for good work. We had to rise to a certain level for an "attaboy," but we did not have to sink to a particularly low level for criticism. I would say on any given week we had an eighty percent chance of receiving more than one "ding" and less than a twenty percent chance of being praised.

If everyone on the crew received one or two "dings," the league office would wrap up the tape by saying, "This crew did not have a very good game." We'd all be lumped in together, and the signal was clear: The crew needed to improve quickly.

Generally, our crew would try to be at our hotel by 6 PM on Friday nights, and we would watch the tape and get it out of the way early because everyone hated it so much. Then we'd go eat dinner together. I saw guys get "dinged" on the tape and be done for the weekend. From that standpoint, it was brutal. We'd come back from dinner and have a meeting that would devolve into a gripe session about the tape.

Some officials would go to bed with the "ding" tape on their mind Friday night, and it would be the first thing they'd think about when they woke up on Saturday morning. I think the league eventually figured out the process was crushing crews mentally, so they later put all the crews on the same tape, and you saw everyone. That didn't work any better. If there was another line judge in trouble, I knew it. And if another line judge was getting "attaboys" every week, I knew that, too. I think that was used to motivate us mentally. After four or five years in the Big 12, I don't know if our techniques got better or if we just didn't need the mind games anymore.

I like to think I had a pretty good attitude about the league's system of providing feedback, because Tim Millis and I were friends. I didn't get beat up a lot, and I possess a certain degree of mental toughness that helped keep it from bothering me when I did. I had the ability to push it out of my mind. I didn't get beat up every week, but when I did, Tim didn't cut me any slack because we were friends. In fact, I think he expected more out of me because we were friends.

The Lord says to those who are given much, much is expected. That is my philosophy when I have problems. No one is perfect. I have been given a lot. I am fortunate. I am blessed. By the same token, a lot is expected of me. That has always been my attitude and the reason I refused to let the Friday night session carry over to Saturday. But I know plenty of guys who did.

Another unpleasant aftereffect of officiating a tough game rears its head on Sundays. If we missed a call or thought we made a questionable call, then the morning after was horrible. We would replay it in our minds and consider what we could have done differently. Of course, we're not the only people doing that. In the Internet age, anyone with a laptop can second-guess an official.

I've never been much on the Internet. I've heard of blogs, but I've never gone and looked at one. In fact, later in my career, particularly after the incident at Baylor in the 1995 season, I stayed away from the media. I learned my lesson the hard way. The media is relentless, and next week it will be someone else in the spotlight.

The only time it doesn't work that way is when you mess up again. Then your previous mistakes come back to haunt you. I tried my best to put a wall between myself and the media during the season as I got older. When I first became an official, I read newspaper articles and tried to learn about every team in the conference. I discovered that once they were writing about me, it wasn't nearly as much fun, so I put the newspapers aside.

Tim never came after us on the tape personally; it was always a 5,000-foot view of officiating. I remember one particular game at Colorado. The receiver who was my key came across the middle. The linebacker literally had him in a bear hug. Meanwhile, the quarterback was trying to decide if he was going to throw the ball. I knew it was going to be a pass play, so I threw a flag for defensive holding. While my flag was in the air, the quarterback threw the ball to my receiver, who did not catch the ball. I told the referee I had defensive holding. The receiver was being tackled, and when I saw that infraction, the ball was not yet in the air. I thought I had made a great call. We penalized ten yards and awarded the offense an automatic first down.

When the "ding" tape came back, the league said it was a terrible call. They wondered why I didn't call pass interference. I saw it as an unquestionable defensive holding call. The league differed. They wanted a fifteen-yard pass interference call because they could still see the holding going on when the ball left the quarterback's hand. The light came on, and it made sense. I was so locked in on defensive holding because the ball hadn't been thrown. They hit me pretty hard on the "ding" tape. That was an example of thinking I had a 100 percent correct call and getting downgraded for making an incorrect call. That was a real learning experience.

I got a few "attaboys" over the years, though. In the Texas–Oklahoma game one season, Texas had the ball on the thirty-yard line and was moving. A running play came toward me with both the center and guard pulling. My key was the tackle, while the umpire had the center and guard. My tackle had sealed off the corner, so I had nothing to do but watch the blocking. The center had two guys wrapped up. All of the traffic in the play kept the umpire from seeing everything that was happening, so when I saw that the center had a defender completely wrapped up, I floated my flag in there and told the referee I had holding. The "ding" tape arrived the next week, and I got an "attaboy" for that call. They thought with the umpire blocked off and me standing there watching the blocking, that it was a great call, even though it wasn't my key. Make that kind of call in a marquee game like Texas–Oklahoma and it's under the microscope. The league wants every call to be correct. The Big 12 does not put marginal officials in that game. If the league thinks the field judge is a marginal official, they will bring in another one. They will not agree with me here, though. They'll tell you that every game is just as important as that one. They will not even admit they have marginal officials on their roster. Anyone who believes that line needs to stay tuned. Texas–Oklahoma is a showpiece game for the league. It usually has national championship implications, and they don't want any mistakes made.

In a game of that magnitude, an official better make sure he's right when he throws his flag, especially if he's flipping the flag in there on someone other than his key. Generally, an official knows right after the game whether he had a good game or not. If not, he can expect to be second-guessed by the graders.

I always had one thing in the back of my mind. The Big 12 told officials that if they had to slow a tape down and run it frame by frame to prove someone wrong, they would not do that. Their plan was to look at all calls in real time and put themselves in the position of the official. That was their philosophy in July. Come November, when coaches would be complaining to the league office about certain calls, we knew they were going to look at them frame by frame. So when we were on our way home after games, one thing we all wondered about was which calls might be put under the magnifying glass.

If we didn't care about what we did and didn't care about getting better and being at the top of the ratings chart, then there was no need to look at those tapes and try to learn from them and improve. The demands of an exhausting weekend take a toll. Imagine how exhausting it is for players and coaches. It's that way for officials, too.

We are out there the entire game, three or more hours, and a lot of officiating goes on between downs. We have a number of responsibilities throughout every game. I don't say that to complain, just to reinforce that we have an intense three or four hours as well, which is not to say it isn't fun. Despite the drudgery, despite the "dings," despite the demands, we still had our share of fun out there.

How couldn't we?

What's the Call?

An ineligible offensive lineman from Team A (Player No. 70) crosses the neutral zone and goes downfield three yards but does not make contact with any opponent. Before quarterback (Player No. 10) throws a legal forward pass, No. 70 returns back across the neutral zone. What's the ruling?

A. No foul, linemen returned behind the neutral zone prior to pass being thrown.

B. No foul because lineman made no contact downfield.

C. Ineligible man downfield, penalize five yards from previous spot plus loss of down.

D. Ineligible man downfield, penalize five yards from previous spot.

(See page 196 for answer.)

CHAPTER FIVE:
BEHIND THE CURTAIN

"A tough day at the office is even tougher when your office contains spectator seating."

—Nik Posa

ANY TIME THE officials huddle, it usually means one of two things: We are working to make sure we have a call right or we are completely stumped about what to do regarding a call one of us has made.

Let me give you an example of the latter. In the 2001 Peach Bowl between Auburn and North Carolina, I made a call that was not in the rulebook. Generally speaking, coaches, players, and league officials frown on that.

Occasionally, though, we have to throw the flag and either work it out or pick it up and wave it off. In this game, North Carolina had the ball and was driving. Tar Heel quarterback Ronald Curry rolled my way for a pass play. Now, on a play like this a lot of things happen quickly, all of which fall on the line judge's plate. I took a couple of easy steps into the backfield when I read pass and began watching the tackle on my side for holding while also keeping an eye on my receiver streaking downfield. As the quarterback rolled my way, I realized I had to get back to the line of scrimmage and keep the down marker on the opposite sideline in my field of vision to accurately judge whether the quarterback threw the ball before crossing the line. That is my responsibility, as well as knowing if the ball actually crossed the line in the air and whether or not it was tipped. The tackle had to be watched for holding, and the receiver had to be allowed to run a pattern without being held. All this is taking place in a time span of about three seconds.

Finally, the quarterback, after almost being pulled to the ground, stepped up and threw the ball toward the sideline. Auburn linebacker Karlos Dansby saw the pass thrown, and right at the sideline, he jumped and intercepted the pass in midair. However, he saw he was going to land out of bounds, which would make the pass incomplete. So once he controlled the ball he threw it forward to teammate Dontarrious Thomas, who caught the ball and was tackled.

I was standing on the sideline thinking that he threw the ball forward. The play was over. All the Auburn players were screaming about an interception. I was certain something was wrong, so I threw my flag knowing that I could always pick it up and wave it off if necessary. Umpire Richard Whittenburg and referee Jon Bible met me at midfield.

"What do you have?" they asked at virtually the same time.

"You're not going to believe this, but the player intercepted the ball and before he came down and completed the catch, he flipped the ball forward."

The rule book did not cover that occurrence for the defense. It was covered for offense only. If the quarterback threw a pass to a receiver, the receiver could catch the ball and flip it forward to another player before landing. Because he has not touched the ground in the field of play in possession of the ball, the pass is not yet completed. Therefore it is not an illegal forward pass or handoff. Common sense says it should work the same way for the defense, but the rules didn't cover that eventuality. The definition of a catch, whether it's a reception or interception, is possession of the ball and one foot in bounds (two feet in the NFL).

I told Jon what happened, and he had a blank look on his face. "That's not in the book," he said.

"What are we going to do now?" I asked.

"Let's kill a little time and watch the replay on the JumboTron," he said.

We huddled there discussing the play and everyone in the stadium, including the officials, is watching the replay. It unfolds exactly as I described. We can't call it a completed pass, but he still flipped the ball forward.

We decided to really mess things up. We allowed Auburn to keep the ball on a completed pass but penalized them five yards for an illegal forward pass. Was it right? No, because it wasn't covered in the rule book, but it also wasn't right to take an interception away from Auburn.

Of course, Auburn was happy to have the ball and didn't care about the penalty. The North Carolina coach wasn't buying it at all. He told us we couldn't give them the ball and penalize them, but we managed to get through it. *Sports Illustrated* ran a short piece about it in its next issue, and every official in America was second-guessing me. To this day, you can still see the play unfold on YouTube.

During the off season, the NCAA rules committee addressed that situation, and our crew felt like a part of rules-making history. Little did Jon and I know we would influence a change in the rulebook before our careers were over.

Having a great rules guy on the crew is critical. Obviously, no official reaches the Division I level without a good working knowledge of the rules, but that book is more than two hundred pages long and contains a lot of fine print. No one possesses the kind of photographic memory to remember every line.

There was one footnote to that game. Tim Millis, the Big 12 supervisor of officials, was in attendance. Typically, he would come to our dressing room before and after games only. He rarely came down at halftime because he didn't want to mess up a crew's focus and momentum. Of course, every media member covering the game in the press box was on Tim. He had a rule book with him, but he couldn't find any rule that addressed that situation, either.

In this instance, he did come to the dressing room at the half. "Don't let that call ruin the game for you," he told us. "It is not addressed and you did the best you could with the situation." He wanted us to know he was supporting us.

On the field, all of that happened, literally, in a few minutes, and that's what it is like to be a college football official in the crosshairs of a controversial call. We spend thousands of hours in meetings, watching film, taking tests, and working games to prepare ourselves for situations like that. If we aren't ready, everyone in the stadium, including our fellow officials, knows it.

When I talk to young officials, they often want to know how to work their way up and receive better game assignments. The only way to do it is through experience. The more seasoned officials get those games. That's the only way to keep from making bad calls. Unfortunately, bad calls give you experience, and the only way to keep from making them is getting experience.

Officials live for one thing, and that is three hours or so of calling a game every Saturday during the fall. But it takes a lot of time, effort, sweat, and tears to get to those Saturdays, and that is what's hardest about it. Summer meetings. Conditioning. Mental preparation. Working scrimmages in August heat. Travel reservations. Figuring out how to get a weekend of clean clothes and officiating gear into your one carry-on bag for the flight.

I carried one bag that was nothing but officiating material. My rules book, mechanics book, notes. I kept every handout in a three-ring binder. That thing takes on a life of its own during the season and has to be reviewed every week. We make notes during every film session. If one of us is criticized by the league office, we track that in our notes. When studying the rulebook or the mechanics book, we continually make new notes. We cover some aspects of the game every week.

We take that mountain of information and try to boil it down and translate it into action on a play that happens in a flash. It's more incredible than any fan might perceive it to be. The level of detail involved and what we're trying to accomplish each and every time we step on the field can be overwhelming. Fans don't see this avalanche of information and the rules interpretations that take place behind the scenes. We have to sort all of that out, interpret it, and apply it. We know it can be done because it happens at all levels of all sports. Basketball officials have to make the block-charge call every game, and many times it can go either way. Plate umpires in baseball make a decision on virtually every pitch, many of which are moving at more than 95 mph.

The men who work college football games represent the middle ground of officiating. They are somewhere between the everyday officials who work high school games and the guys who get paid a lot of money to do it in the NFL. Regardless, the expectation of coaches and fans are the same. They want it perfect. Every time. All the time.

And we can't quit our day jobs to do this. Officials are employed, have families, and lead somewhat normal lives, although I'm sure life for most college football officials is not the same as life for everybody else. For balance, I think we should all have another hobby. Some guys play golf. I like working on my ranch. All of us have our regular callings. From the standpoint of being the CEO of City Bank Texas and making the calls that have to be made in that chair, officiating was pretty easy for me.

The officiating schedule required compressing the workweek into four days because we would return from the game late Sunday afternoon and were flying back out either Thursday evening or Friday morning. In my case, with outside board meetings and the functions that my schedule required, each fall was packed full.

All the things I had to do between Monday morning and packing time Thursday night created a situation where there was not enough of me to go around. Something was going to have to suffer or be neglected, and in my case, I felt like it was going to be officiating. I could get by with that for a little while with the level of experience

I had, but no one can get away with it very long. Preparation is an important aspect of what it takes to get to Saturday afternoon. To offset this, in my opinion, would be significant pay increases for college football officials, but I will come back to that later.

I always found one of the best times to study and prepare was on the airplane on the way to the game site, and some of the best preparation the crew has once we reach the site is talking among ourselves. Our crew's philosophy was to be totally focused on the coming game when we arrived on Friday. That's virtually all we talked about. We might spend a little time catching up on what everyone did the previous week, but it didn't take long for our conversation to turn to rules situations.

We would try to stump each other. What about this play? What about this situation? Invariably someone would come across a situation no one else had covered in their preparation. Then we would talk about those unusual plays and see who was ready for any eventuality. By the time we were through talking, we all were.

If we had a late kickoff on Saturday, the Friday night pregame would be pretty relaxed. If the kickoff was early, 1 PM or before, we had a pretty intense pregame session the night before and we were up early the next morning. For instance, the first time I worked a Texas–Oklahoma game, which is almost always a 2:30 PM start, we had our normal Friday night routine and then planned to be at the stadium two full hours before kickoff.

That meant allowing time for travel to the stadium and having lunch before leaving. When the start time is that early, we get pregame going quickly. I learned an important lesson one year at that game. We had a quick lunch and got in our cars to travel to the stadium, figuring we'd be at the Cotton Bowl by 12:30 PM. Then we got stuck in traffic for two hours with everyone else trying to get there two hours early. We arrived at the stadium in time to dress and walk out on the field, which wasn't much fun.

In many cases, we'd have breakfast and start the pregame routine. Some stadiums are set up for us to have our pregame there. They have a meeting room set up with refreshments and a table where we can meet. I liked getting to the stadium really early and having pregame. We could sit around in a T-shirt and not wear shoes. That gave us a chance to relax and focus. One thing a lot of people may not know is that the Big 12 has an observer who sits with the crew through pregame to watch that crew prepare. An observer travels with every crew, and I always wonder what's going on in their minds while we're going through our rituals.

Sometimes the observer would go to dinner with us, and sometimes we wouldn't see him until we began pregame. The conference always sends the referee a personnel list that identifies the observer, the game administrator, the time keeper, and the crew members. The conference has specific people assigned to specific roles each game, and each game is a little different. At some games, there are people are just hanging around in an officially unofficial capacity. Other games, depending on their magnitude, might have two or three conference representatives or the league commissioner attending.

For instance, our crew has traveled to Penn State and Florida State, and the seven on our crew didn't see a soul from the conference the whole weekend. We all flew in from different places, arrived at the hotel, and managed to get to the stadium the next day on our own.

We typically begin pregame after breakfast, and it has a specific format. We break pregame into what we do before the game, outside elements such as television, radio, or other special events, and timing. We discuss who will be on the field to observe the teams during their warm-ups and how the field is broken up for warm-ups. After all, we're talking about college kids, and they would take up the entire field if we let them. If we were dealing with a big-time rivalry, and a couple of players were out there looking for trouble, the warm-up session is the time this can happen. We are there to try and keep the peace so we can start the game without a penalty. The crew officially takes control of the game from one hour before kickoff until the game is over, and can call and enforce penalties throughout that entire period. If an infraction occurred before kickoff, most likely it would be an unsportsmanlike conduct foul, and we would enforce the penalty on the opening kickoff.

During pregame, we cover all aspects of the kicking game, running plays, passing plays, scoring plays. We cover what will happen between quarters, during the half, and at the end of the game. We spend time talking through every scenario. For instance, if we work a game at

Texas A&M, where they have a tremendous march-in of their military corps before the game, we have to be out there to make sure a visiting player doesn't interfere with this process. We had a brawl once in the Southwest Conference before a Texas–Texas A&M game even started.

I have to admit, though, sitting through pregame ten or eleven weeks in a row, it can become a stale process by that eleventh week. Our crew worked to avoid that by assigning a different member to be in charge of pregame each week, so each crew member might oversee pregame only a couple of times each season. That way, we had a fresh voice and a fresh perspective, particularly for those situations out of the ordinary that seemed to pop up a couple of times each season.

The referee began the process by covering the logistics and travel for the next week so that was out of the way early. He talked about who would be responsible for renting the car and what time everyone would arrive at the airport. Someone would arrive first, get the car, and pick up everyone else by a certain time. It is an easier process today because of e-mail, but in the old days that was a base you wanted covered.

After that, someone on the crew would oversee the pregame and ensure they covered anything out of the ordinary. If I was in charge, I might do a presentation over some aspect of the rules that I had not studied in a while or something that I had spent time studying but wasn't as comfortable with as I would like.

We discussed punts and the mechanics of what would happen if the ball was snapped over the punter's head or if the team ran a fake punt or if the receiving team ran a reverse on its return. The idea is to bring up something that is a possibility and make it interesting. Our crew tried another pregame approach once and had each person responsible for a portion. One member would cover the running game one week and the passing game the next week.

A crew member would discuss the differences between the passing game and the airborne game. How is the airborne game different? Passing is throwing the ball. An example of the airborne game occurs when Receiver A is airborne, penetrates the goal line, is knocked back, and fumbles the ball. Is that a touchdown? The answer is no because the receiver has not touched the ground with possession of the ball in the field of play or the end zone. If he fumbled the ball without touching the ground, the ruling is an incomplete pass.

We spent time talking about momentum, but not the kind teams generate from executing big plays. In this case, a more apt example would be when a deep receiver misjudges a kickoff and it goes over his head. He catches the ball at the one-yard line, and his momentum then takes him into the end zone where he downs the ball. Because he possessed it at the one-yard line, that's where I throw my beanbag, letting the crew know we have a momentum play. The one-yard line is where the ball will next be put in play. It does not come out to the twenty-yard line as the result of a touchback.

What do we talk about during a four-hour pregame? Those are typical examples of our discussions. Once we finish pregame, we might have a test. The pregame routine depends entirely on the referee. Some newer referees might have a longer pregame than those who are more seasoned. Our pregames were usually a minimum of two hours, and that followed the Friday night session. If we were working a Saturday night game, we would meet for ninety minutes that morning, have lunch, and then do another ninety minutes. After that, we might watch a little bit of a game on television, gather our stuff, and head to the stadium. Much of it hinges on travel time to the stadium and other variables.

Everyone is relieved once pregame winds down. We've spent the week building up for the game, traveled, seen film, and had Friday night pregame and Saturday pregame. If we don't know our stuff by now, we never will. So let's work the game.

We're familiar with most of the stadiums in which we work games, and once we get there we begin our rituals. Some guys stretch. Some guys put on headphones and listen to music. Some guys lie around and meditate. Some like to talk. To that extent, we're probably like players in the fact that once we get to the dressing room, no one wants to be messed with.

Usually, the referee and umpire dress quickly because they visit the head coaches seventy-five minutes before kickoff. The line judge and back judge are typically the first two to go out onto the field, and that's sixty minutes before kickoff. I've always seen that as a good thing because I like to get out of the dressing room after being cooped up for hours in pregame. I want to walk around and become acclimated to the surroundings. My impression has always been that fans arriving early think officials are silly walking around the stadium like that.

Personally, there's something about getting acclimated, knowing which way is north and which way is south, that helped me focus on the task at hand. I liked to make sure the pylons were in the right place. I walked up the sideline at the end of the end zone, and I always did that on the sideline where I was going to work. By the way, the line judge always works the press box sideline.

I found it helpful to walk around stadiums where I hadn't worked before, but I did it every week, regardless of whether I had been there previously. At Oklahoma State, for example, if you're at the goal line near the pylons, and the play is moving toward the pylon, the mechanics tell you to back straight up. However, at that stadium, it's only about six feet from the pylons to the concrete wall. I don't care how many times you've been there and worked—and I worked a couple of dozen games there—I always went to that goal line and backed up as part of my preparation. I wanted a sense of where the wall was. An official can get hurt at that goal line.

The sidelines are always a little different, as well, and I always wanted a feel for where I was going to be. I wanted to know how the grass was and how I could cut on it and how much room I had when I needed to step. Sure, those are small things, but when trying to be the best official possible at that level, the little things add up to huge advantages.

I wanted a sense of what the surface was like, too. With the advent of new FieldTurf, which is a uniform product, you will still find differences from stadium to stadium. Kansas's turf is different from Nebraska's, and Floyd Casey Stadium, where Baylor plays, had the first version of that turf, which is different from each of those. Some fields are grass, and some have artificial turf. Every place is a little different, even the locations of the 25-second clocks. The field judge and back judge have to know where those clocks are because they are responsible for watching them.

On my sideline, I wanted a feel for where the game clock was located. The line judge checks the clock before and after every play to make sure it is running or not running, depending on the outcome of the play. We have to be able to know where the clock is, and we can't make a big deal out of it. Once a play is over, we can't take our concentration away from that pile of players. We make a casual look at the clock for a second. It has to be a smooth motion that keeps our focus on the field.

By the time the umpire and referee return from their meetings with the head coaches, the head linesman is on the field talking to the chain crew. With twenty minutes left before kickoff, the teams must leave the field. That gives the bands time to perform and allows for any final pregame ceremonies planned by the host school. That's when we go back into our dressing room. We have five or six minutes for one final meeting. Two or three things happen during that time. The referee and the umpire will go over any unusual plays that the respective coaches have mentioned. Crew members talk about players who had uniform problems such as too many towels on their belt, something written on their jersey, a cast that was not checked. We get those issues cleared up then. Our philosophy was to talk to players about equipment infractions. We would rather tell the player without penalizing the team.

If a team has fourteen guys without knee pads and pants above the knee, we let the coach know not to send them in or we'll send them right back out. In reality, once the game starts, we don't have time to look at equipment because we have a lot of other responsibilities. During the game our goal is to get the big stuff right and not worry about the nitpicky stuff.

Then we go back out and get the teams on the field. The line judge and field judge bring the team out on their side of the field. The back judge and side judge bring the other team out on their side of the field. We go to the dressing room, and the field judge brings out the team captains while I stay back with the team. We have a sheet that details exactly what will happen in the time leading up to kickoff.

However, coaches being how they are, we never know what might happen. A coach could decide to send everyone out with the captains. If that happens, we have a TV producer who isn't going to be happy because that spoils one of their signature shots: a team racing onto the field for combat. They want the team standing in the tunnel and coming out the way it's choreographed. One thing I was careful about during my career was to avoid coming out with the team. I never went through the human tunnel lined with students and the band. My job as escort was over once the team reached the face of the tunnel.

Leading the team out to play is a great experience. I remember bringing the Fighting Irish out at Notre Dame. Talk about unbelievable. In 1989, when Texas Tech played at Texas, I was in charge of bringing the Texas Longhorns out. The field judge and I walked down there to bring the captains out. Just outside the Texas dressing room, I saw head coach David McWilliams. He told me to go in and get them.

I walked into the dressing room, and standing in the locker room giving a pep talk was Nolan Ryan, one of the greatest pitchers of all time. By the time I got into the dressing room, I was about fifteen seconds away from being late. I figured when he saw me walk in, he'd stop. Finally, I told him we had to go, so I'm one of the few people ever to interrupt a Nolan Ryan pep talk.

When I was bringing the Houston Cougars out of their locker room one year, I wound up walking out of the dressing room with Carl Lewis, the great Olympic champion. I thought that would be the perfect time to see if he wanted to race, but he didn't.

The sidelines are a great place to see famous faces. Baseball great Roger Clemens and I had a running conversation one year when I was working the Texas sideline. During timeouts, I'd turn around and talk to him. Years later, when I attended a Major League All-Star Game in Houston, I was fortunate enough to have breakfast with him and we had our photograph taken. Each time I visited with Roger, it was an enjoyable experience.

Paul Hornung, one of the all-time great Notre Dame players, was on the Fighting Irish sideline when I worked a game there, and it was great to meet him. He had the biggest hands of any I had ever shaken. When I worked the Oklahoma–Kansas State Big 12 Championship Game in Kansas City, I ran into Brian Bosworth, the former Sooner All-American, on the sideline.

I had met him several times before, and we recognized each other. He was standing over there with a cowboy-looking guy with holes in his jeans. I walked over and shook Bosworth's hand, but I didn't know who the other guy was. A friend of mine watching on television told me later that I was not only talking to Bosworth, but also country music superstar Toby Keith. I later learned that Keith is a huge Sooners fan. Of course, at that time, I just thought he was part of Bosworth's entourage, and I probably still wouldn't recognize Toby Keith if I saw him today.

One of my biggest thrills came before a Texas–Texas A&M game when I was honored to meet former president George H.W. Bush. I walked up and introduced myself to him, despite the fact that he had what looked to me to be Secret Service men all around him. That was interesting because I don't think many people can walk right up and shake a former president's hand, but if you're wearing a black-and-white striped shirt, I guess it's all right. A photographer was there, and he snapped a picture of President Bush and me. A few weeks later, I received an autographed copy of that photo in the mail. Talk about a memory.

Of course, all this happens *before* the game. Once the action starts, we're all business. We get the teams on the field and toss the coin. One of the things the line judge is responsible for is bringing in the football to be used for the kickoff. Whenever a change of possession occurs during the game, the new football comes in from the line judge side as well. I have the responsibility of turning to the ball boys and requesting the team's ball to be used each possession.

The other six officials are already out there, and the line judge usually is the last one to come onto the field. He pitches the ball to the umpire. That is always a special time for an officiating crew. Teams are on their respective sidelines, getting their kicking and receiving teams together, depending on which team won the toss. If fans watch closely, they will see the officials also get together in a little huddle. Each one will put a hand on the ball, and someone will say something like, "Let's go have some fun and have a great game," or, "Let's get this game in the record book where it belongs."

I've even had a little prayer out there. Generally, we have our prayer in the dressing room before we go out. When that huddle breaks, fans might see some officials, all fired up, running to their positions. I always walked. One reason is you have a lot of time before the kickoff while the last commercials are running on TV. I also think it sends a clear signal of confidence when we calmly walk to our positions and wait for the kickoff.

The biggest relief is when we see that opening kickoff in the air. That's the same for us as it is for players and coaches. We want the game to start smoothly and flow smoothly throughout.

That gets an official's motor running.

What's the Call?

First and ten for Team A from Team B's twenty-yard line. On a legal forward pass play, Team B player intercepts deep in his own end zone and advances but does not get out of the end zone, where he is downed. After the interception and during the attempted runback, Team B clips Team A in the end zone. What is the ruling?

A. Team B keeps ball after penalty from previous spot. First and ten for Team B from its own ten.

B. Team A declines the penalty and keeps the ball and replays the down.

C. Safety, award Team A two points.

(See page 196 for answer.)

CHAPTER SIX: DOUBLE T TROUBLE

"I'd rather be a communist than an official."

—Spike Dykes, former head coach, Texas Tech University

OFFICIALS DO THEIR best work when they are neither seen nor heard, and they've done a particularly good job if they're not remembered. Rest assured, no official wants his legacy to be a controversial call that turned out to be incorrect. Officials, whatever the sport, have done a great job if they performed without being noticed.

That said, I always had a difficult time not being noticed whenever I worked a Texas Tech game.

Longtime fellow official Richard Whittenburg said it best: "If Liner has a Texas Tech game, sooner or later, trouble will find him."

One truism about officials: We do not like calling games close to home. During the first part of my career in the Southwest Conference, it didn't matter because I wasn't living in Lubbock. I lived about an hour away in Morton, but I was a member of the local officials' chapter and I worked my share of Texas Tech scrimmages so I could see college football plays at full-speed. The more snaps an official sees, the better that official becomes, even if some of those snaps occur in practice.

The irony of it all is that being assigned a Texas Tech game is the dream of every football official within 200 miles of Lubbock. We work high school games and small college games just hoping for a chance to be assigned a game at Jones AT&T Stadium. And we wonder how we will do in a pressure situation with 50,000 people watching. We wonder if we have the guts to do it and stand up to the pressure. Some games eventually come down to a crucial point where an official either makes a call or doesn't, and that always seemed to happen to me when I called Tech games.

I got my first chance to officiate a Texas Tech home game during non-conference play in the 1989 season, when I was assigned to work the New Mexico–Texas Tech game. I wasn't as uncomfortable calling Tech games then because at that time most people in Lubbock didn't know me and didn't care that a guy from Morton was working the game. The fact that I lived there didn't mean any more than if I had been living in any other surrounding town.

In the dressing room prior to a Baylor vs. Texas A&M game at Kyle Field, back judge Randy McAnally (left), referee Tom Ahlers, and I discuss receiver coverages as seen on the whiteboard in the background.

This was the first Big 12 crew of which I was a part. This shot was taken during the league's first season in 1996 at Sanford Stadium prior to Texas Tech facing Georgia. The crew (from left to right) was field judge Rick Johnson, side judge Phil Laurie, umpire Richard Whittenburg, referee Bud Alexander, head linesman Mark Hitner, line judge Mike Liner, and back judge Mark (Luther) Johnson.

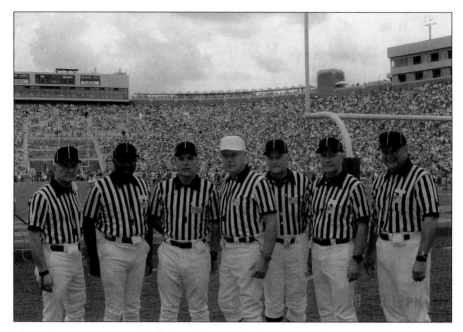

This Big 12 crew worked the non-conference game between Colorado and Florida State in Tallahassee, Florida. Shown (from left to right) are line judge Mike Liner, head linesman Curtis Graham, field judge Jim Hatfield, referee John Laurie, umpire Richard Whittenburg, back judge John Robison, and side judge Tom Walker.

This photo illustrates the wisdom of officials getting off the field as soon as the game is over. Here we are leaving the chaos at Folsom Field in Boulder, Colorado, following a Colorado–Colorado State battle.

A pregame shot of the Southwest Conference crew that officiated the 1994 Liberty Bowl between East Carolina and Illinois in Memphis, Tennessee. Crew members were line judge Mike Liner, head linesman Don Brown, field judge Jon Bible, back judge Ron Murphy, referee Lloyd Dale, umpire Jerry Marlar, and side judge John Lewis.

Texas coach Mack Brown makes his case after a facemask call against his team during the Longhorns' Big 12 game against Kansas State. Obviously, Coach Brown disagrees with guys wearing the striped shirts.

Coach Brown and I were getting along better in this shot, taken at the Black Tie and Boots Ball in Washington, D.C. during the presidential inauguration celebration of George W. Bush in 2001.

Field judge Jeff Lambert and I hold a brief conversation during a timeout in a 1999 home game at Nebraska. In the background (besides Herbie Husker) is back judge Lynn Williams.

The Oklahoma State mascot joined our crew for this pregame shot in 2005. Crew members (from left to right) were line judge Mike Liner, referee Tom Walker, side judge Jim Hatfield, head linesman Curtis Graham, umpire Hugh Douglas, Derrick Rhone-Dunn, and back judge Mark (Luther) Johnson.

Oklahoma head coach Bob Stoops always had time for a pre-game conversation.

Supervisor of officials Tim Millis (far right) with the Big 12 crew that worked the 2006 Gator Bowl between Louisville and Virginia Tech. Back judge Brad Van Vark, umpire Rusty Weir, field judge Greg Burks, referee Steve Usechek, line judge Mike Liner, side judge Scott (Scooter) Koch, head linesman Al Green, and alternate official Joe Pester.

It was my unpleasant duty to tell coach Gene Stallings that his team had been penalized, wiping out a big play for the Crimson Tide in the 1993 Sugar Bowl, that season's national championship game.

Our crew in the officials' parking lot before a game in 2001 between defending national champion Oklahoma and Air Force. The crew (from left to right) is line judge Mike Liner, referee Tom Ahlers, side judge Duane Osborne, head linesman Curtis Graham, back judge Mark (Luther) Johnson, umpire Jim Jankowski, and field judge Scott Gaines.

DOYLE JACKSON'S CREW 1991

My 1991 Southwest Conference crew. This picture was taken at the SWC meeting in Houston. Back row (left to right) head linesman Gary Slaughter, field judge Randy Christal, umpire Bill Voss, referee Doyle Jackson. Front row (left to right) line judge Mike Liner, back judge Larry Weeks, part-time side judge Ed Kentig, and full-time side judge Tom Moore. Jackson and Weeks were former NFL officials, and Moore and Slaughter were soon to be NFL officials.

This excerpt appeared in *Sports Illustrated* following a ruling our crew made in the 2001 Peach Bowl.

SPORTS ILLUSTRATED
JANUARY 7, 2002

The 1993 Sugar Bowl crew prior to kickoff between Alabama and Miami. Crew members (left to right) were line judge Mike Liner, referee Rogers Redding, back judge Ron Murphy, field judge Jon Bible, umpire Joe Darden, side judge Mike Wetzel, and head linesman Gary Slaughter. Also pictured is the clock operator.

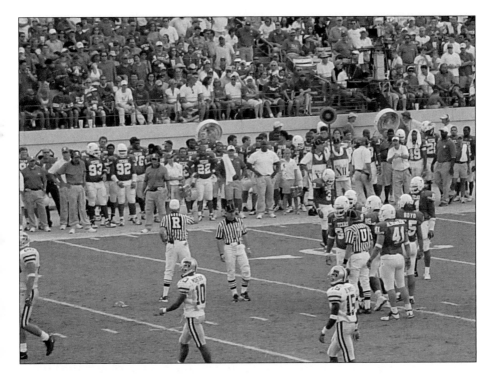

Anytime your flag hits the ground in Austin, you can expect a bit of animated conversation. Referee John Laurie is in the process of giving a preliminary signal as a result of my flag during this game between the Longhorns and Kansas State.

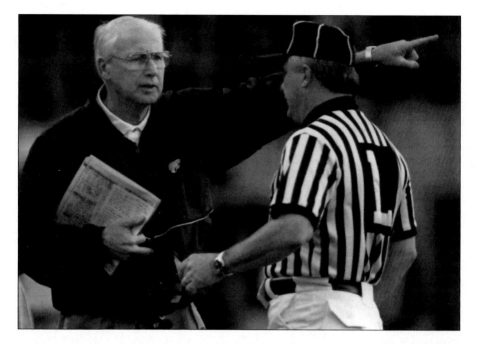

Kansas State coach Bill Snyder reacts after learning of his team's infraction during a game against Nebraska in Lincoln. I'm sure he's not showing me the way to heaven.

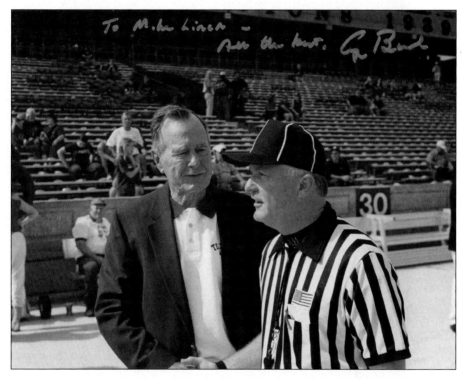

You never know who you might meet on the sidelines before a game. I was fortunate enough to shake hands with former president George H.W. Bush before this game at Texas A&M.

National Football Foundation

Longtime fellow official Jim Schiermeyer (right) introduced me prior to my receiving the outstanding football official award from the Texas Tech chapter of the National Football Foundation and College Hall of Fame in 2004.

We're in the middle of a pregame meeting in the officials' dressing room at Memorial Stadium in Lincoln. Besides reviewing game possibilities on John Laurie's roll-up football field (as seen on the table), crew members watching film are (from left) Richard Whittenburg, Brad Horchem, me, and Phil Laurie.

College officiating mechanics in action as Oklahoma's Adrian Peterson scores from 6 yards out. That's me at the 5-yard line, watching the blocking at the point of attack. Field judge Greg Burks, responsible for the goal line, is backing away from the pylon to increase his field of vision on the play.

I crossed paths with my old friend, U.S. Senator Phil Gramm of Texas, a Texas A&M alum, on the sidelines at Oklahoma State prior to this game between the Aggies and the Cowboys.

The game was going along pretty well until the fourth quarter, when trouble knocked on my door. Tech was ahead a few points, and New Mexico was driving. The Lobos moved the ball close to Tech's goal line, and they had to score a touchdown to take the lead. When fourth down rolled around, they had to go for it because a field goal wouldn't help.

New Mexico quarterback Jeremy Leach took the snap and started rolling toward my sideline although he was deep in the backfield. The snap took place inside the seven-yard line, and the mechanics called for me to get to the goal line immediately after the snap. I was watching the play. Tech was pressuring the quarterback, and Leach kept rolling out to buy time. I was watching both my receiver and the blocking at the line of scrimmage, all the while knowing that any goal line call would be mine. My boat was loaded.

When the quarterback reached the sideline he realized he had no room and no receivers, so he cut upfield and headed for the pylon at the corner of the end zone. I saw him coming and forgot everything else because I had the goal line responsibility, and I had to keep that in front of me.

Goal line mechanics call for the covering official to back straight up from the pylon, giving plenty of room for action at the pylon while keeping the goal line in view. Leach planted his foot on the sideline, cut upfield and dived for the goal line. I remember seeing him in the air and thinking, "He has the ball." He was headed for the goal line, but just before he arrived, a Tech linebacker roared out of the end zone and collided with him right at the goal line. It was a heck of a hit. The pylon disappeared, and I judged the ball to be out of bounds about six inches short of the goal line.

I signaled it was Tech's ball, and the Raiders took over on downs.

It was such a close call. I had a sixth sense about where the ball was on that play, and it became a topic of conversation throughout the next few days.

Now, here's the rest of the story. When Leach ran out of room at the sideline and planted his foot, his toe was out of bounds, which made the goal-line collision and all the drama afterward inconsequential. Neither the referee nor I saw that. The quarterback was the referee's responsibility until crossing the line of scrimmage. I was a hair away from calling that play a touchdown. Had that happened, New Mexico probably would have won the game, and game films would have confirmed that the play should not have been called a touchdown. Had I ruled that a score, my SWC career probably would have been substantially shorter.

On a play like that, the referee is trailing a running quarterback so if he does step out of bounds, as was the case here, he can help coordinate where the ball should be spotted. The unwritten rule is that the referee watches the quarterback as long as he has the ball. That does not relieve me from the responsibility of the runner stepping on the sideline even if it occurs back upfield. I was young with little experience in this type of situation and that day my thought process was focused on the goal line and not on the sideline. However, the Lord was looking out for me that day.

For the rest of my career, I can guarantee that when I had the goal line, I paid attention to the sideline up the field. I learned a lesson on that play. The way I handled that particular call from that day forward was to work the goal line, work the sideline, and look back to the trailing official before signaling a touchdown.

That moment was typical of what invariably happened whenever I was part of the crew for a Texas Tech game in Lubbock. I officiated Red Raider games in Austin, College Station, Houston, Waco, San Antonio, Lincoln, and other points and never had a problem. My situation was not uncommon, either, as other officials around the league regularly worked games in their own hometowns. Jon Bible and Randy Christal lived in Austin and handled Texas games. Al Green was a Missouri official who worked games involving the Tigers.

By the time the Big 12 emerged, I was living in Lubbock and working as CEO of City Bank Texas. I never made a big deal about calling Texas Tech games when I first got in the league because I was happy to be there. I knew I could do it, and I didn't want to ask for any special dispensation and end up having someone second-guess me.

Tim Millis, the Big 12 supervisor of officials, never perceived it to be a problem for any of his officials. He knew no reputable official would bust his tail for twenty years to reach the Division I level and then surrender his reputation to be a homer. Personally, I had worked too hard to get where I was to throw it away as a Texas Tech homer. The same is true with every Division I football official with whom I have ever worked. So from that standpoint, Tim knew his officials weren't going to be lenient toward one school just because of where they happened to live.

For whatever reason, tough calls came my way virtually every time I worked a Tech game on the South Plains of Texas. In the first year of the Big 12, Tech and Texas were playing in Lubbock. The Red Raiders were putting together a pretty impressive second-half comeback after being down and out in the opening half. I was the line judge, and Tech threw a long pass down my sideline toward the end zone. The field judge was in the correct position, standing on the goal line just outside the pylon, and my job was to move down the sideline and help in this particular situation.

As it turned out, the Texas defensive back hooked Tech's receiver in the end zone at an angle that prevented the field judge from seeing it. I was moving down the sideline at about the thirty-yard line, and this play—obviously pass interference—took place right in front of the field judge. I saw what happened, but it wasn't my primary area of responsibility. I was thinking, "He will throw the flag," but he didn't. So instinctively, I did. The field judge walked over and asked me what I had, and I told him it was pass interference against Texas in the end zone.

The call set Tech up with a first down at the Texas one-yard line, and the Red Raiders went on to score. Tech failed to prevail in that game, and I can't tell you how quiet the ride back to the hotel was because I had thrown a flag in front of another experienced official during a game in Lubbock, where I live. When the game tape arrived the next week, I was told I undoubtedly made the correct call, but the voiceover on the tape wondered why I was so far out of position. In so many words, that was the league's way of saying they didn't like one official throwing a flag in another official's jurisdiction. I wasn't sure how to read that. I thought I was supposed to provide backup on a play like that. Maybe the league meant nothing by it, but I was sensitive to what I perceived as criticism.

The next time I found myself surrounded by controversy was in a Tech game against Missouri. It was Halloween, 1998, and it was a day for crazy weather in Lubbock. We had a north wind strong enough to blow small children out of their seats. Then we had snow and, oddly enough, lightning, which caused referee John Lewis to delay the game's start about thirty minutes. The Raiders and Tigers were playing a close game. Missouri had the ball near midfield in the opening quarter moving into that strong north wind. Missouri quarterback Corby Jones ran an option play toward me on the Tech sideline, and the Raiders surrounded him and began dragging him down. As Jones dropped to his knees and went down, he pitched the ball to running back Devin West, who failed to catch the ball, and Tech recovered what it thought was a fumble. Actually, in officials' speak, it was a muffed backward pass.

There was only one problem. I had already called the quarterback down. His knee touched the turf before he pitched the ball. Tech coach Spike Dykes moved down the sideline close enough to tell me it was the worst call he'd ever seen, and the Tech fans were really letting me have it. All the time, I was thinking to myself that I had the call right. One truism of Big 12 officiating is this: Never give away a cheap fumble. If a runner is down, he is down. I was confident the call was correct. As it turned out, Tech lost the game, Spike was an unhappy coach, and he was unhappy about a lot more than that one call.

Again, we received a critiqued game tape the following week. The voiceover indicated the line judge (me) used incorrect judgment on the pitch because the quarterback's knee was two inches off the ground. In my defense, I have to say for the league office to have noticed that, they had to have examined that replay frame by frame. The following frame showed the quarterback's knee down and the ball just released. The knee touching and the ball leaving his hand were, literally, a thousandth of a second apart, but I was trying to stick to the league's philosophy and not give up a cheap fumble.

I wonder what might have happened if the pitchman had caught the ball on that play. It probably would have changed Spike's verbiage. It was one of those calls where, depending on what happened, one team and its fans were going to be upset regardless of the call made. If the play went off as designed, and the pitchman didn't drop the ball, fans would have been mad because he should have been ruled down. Again, it all depends on one's angle and perspective. If Missouri executed on that play, Tech would have had a different argument to make. Missouri didn't execute, and the line judge turned out to be the bad guy.

Tech pleaded its case to the Big 12, and one of the things the Big 12 always told us was if the league had to run a film frame by frame to prove an official incorrect, it wouldn't happen because officials are making those calls in real time. However, they would run a play frame by frame to prove an official correct. In this case, looking at it frame by frame, I was incorrect—by a gnat's hair.

Did that call decide the game? I doubt it, although it was a close contest in which the Tigers claimed a 28–26 victory. However, Missouri was the superior team on that particular day as Tech had three fumbles that led to Tiger touchdowns. It was an especially tough loss for Tech as it marked the third straight week that the Raiders had dropped a decision by seven points or fewer. I admit, after frame by frame analysis, I was incorrect. Looking at it in full speed would persuade most people to agree with my call. If someone asked the other men on the crew about that call, they would, to a man, say it was correct.

That still wasn't the pinnacle of how Double T Trouble always seemed to find me. The all-timer came in a Tech–Kansas State game on November 1, 1997.

That Tech–Kansas State game was important from several perspectives. The Wildcats were ranked in the top five along with Nebraska that week and they had a quarterback, Michael Bishop, who was among the best in the nation. Tech was trying to earn a victory against one of the tougher teams from the old Big Eight. Add to this the fact that the Big 12, only in its second year and was still establishing its identity on the college football landscape, had a chance to send not just one but two teams to a BCS Bowl if K-State and Nebraska stayed undefeated the rest of the way.

The Raiders had knocked off nationally ranked Texas A&M with a late field goal in a 16–13 victory the previous week, and a second consecutive win against a Top 25 program would have given Tech a nice boost heading into the final month of the season. Kansas State, meanwhile, had lost only once, and that was to Nebraska. The Wildcats ventured onto the South Plains and struggled throughout the game. Tech stuggled as well, scoring its only points on a first-quarter safety.

Bishop, a gifted quarterback, engineered a touchdown drive late in the first half but failed on a two-point conversion try, resulting in the somewhat unusual halftime score of 6–2. The Raiders kept battling away. They were game, and K-State was, for whatever reason, not on the mark. The Wildcats, who had a truly superb defense, were hanging in there. Then, in the fourth quarter, Tech got an interception and returned it inside the Kansas State ten yard line. Down by four, the Raiders had to score a touchdown to win.

Out came the Tech offense led by Zebbie Lethridge, who grew up in Lubbock and was a great multi-sport star before signing with Tech and becoming the starting quarterback as a true freshman during the 1994 season. He was a senior now, so he had been in these types of situations before. Tech ran a play up the middle that didn't gain much, but it did push the Raiders a bit closer to the end zone.

On the next play, Tech decided to run a quarterback sneak. He dived toward the end zone and stretched the ball out toward the goal line. From where I was, I plainly saw that the ball was broken the plane of the goal line. Zebbie stretched into the pile holding up the ball, which is like holding up raw meat in front of a pack of hungry dogs. I remember thinking, *There's the ball.* It was like a magnet, drawing everyone toward it. The ball had still not penetrated the goal line, and suddenly it disappeared into a swarm of people. And then the ball was rolling free in the end zone.

We had a great crew that day. Al Green was the head linesman, J.C. Leimbach was the umpire, and I was the line judge. We were the three officials destined to rule on what had quickly become anything but a simple quarterback sneak. J.C. is from St. Joe, Missouri, and Al's hometown is Columbia, Missouri, so none of us had any ties to Kansas State. We had two teams, a ball rolling free in the end zone, and a Kansas State player eventually landing on it. Al and I were at the pylons, because once the ball was snapped, we moved to the goal line for a clear view of whether the ball broke the plane or not. I saw the ball in the air, saw it disappear out of Zebbie's hands, and saw a Kansas State player come up with it in the end zone.

I knew I had to rule. My officiating instincts told me Zebbie fumbled the ball into the end zone. I moved in on the play looking at the head linesman and the umpire. If Al had a touchdown, he would plainly signal it. If J.C. had a touchdown, he would be nodding his head at me because the procedure is for the umpire never to signal a touchdown but to let the officials on the line of scrimmage make that call. The head linesman made no movement, however, and the umpire looked right down the goal line at me. I waved my arm indicating it was a touchback, and they both said they had the same thing. Of the three of us, I had the best look at the play.

Of course, Spike was really upset. The game film was sent to the Big 12 office, and before it was ever sent there, I'm sure Tech looked at it from every angle to see if that was a touchdown or not. When I saw the game film, I saw the ball and the shadow of the ball outside the goal line. The supervisor said they looked at that play from every angle. When they finished reviewing it, I was told two things:

1) I was the only official in position to make that call on that play.

2) The shadow of the ball is short of the goal line.

The supervisor said he could not see any evidence that the ball had broken the plane. Everyone watching the game in Lubbock tried to put it in the end zone, and there I was, a Lubbock official. The supervisor told me, "I think you got it right." Later that season, I was named line judge for the Big 12 Championship game.

In the aftermath of all these stories, I developed something of an unwanted and undeserved reputation, at least in the eyes of several Texas Tech officials. Athletic Director Gerald Myers, current Tech football coach Mike Leach, and, I'm sure, a few others, believe I will go out of my way not to make a call for Tech because I feel so prejudiced for them. Consequently, they do not want me working their games, and each took steps to try to see that one of my fellow officials (also from Lubbock) and I didn't.

Let me tell you about officials playing favorites. We can't and don't do it. Any official prejudiced toward a team would have his bias show up long before a big call in a big game. Not many times will an official have as many big calls come his way as I did in Texas Tech games. It was just one of those things. Maybe it was the Lord saying, "When are you going to listen to me and quit going out there?"

A biased official is going to show favoritism spotting the ball, on a holding call, or on something like that long before the big call. I've never seen anything along those lines at the Division I level. Sometimes things just work out that way. I'm sure everyone has seen a football game in which one team is called for six or seven infractions before the other team is called for one. That's sports. I've worked games in which it looked like the officials were calling everything against one team, but that's just the way it happened to work out in that particular game.

I had no intention of sacrificing my Big 12 career, my name, and my reputation for Texas Tech or anyone else. I might miss a call. I might make a wrong decision. But I am never going to compromise my integrity. I never had a Texas coach or a Nebraska coach or any other coach accuse me of hawking for Texas Tech; the only problems

I had were from Tech. By the way, I also made a number of calls that happened to go Tech's way.

Case in point: Texas running back Ricky Williams just seemed to run wild against Tech, and the 1996 game between the teams was no exception. In this case, he was running free in the Tech secondary on a play that began in Texas territory. Two Red Raiders jumped on his back, causing him to drag his knee around the thirty-yard line. He got up and ran for a touchdown, but I blew the play dead where his knee touched about the time he was crossing the goal line. Texas eked out a 38–32 victory, and the game tape the next week indicated I was correct, although it insisted I made the call from a long ways away.

Officials work very hard for a long time to have a chance to be part of Division I football games. From a personal standpoint, why would any official jeopardize years of hard work reaching the Division I level by purposely trying to give one team an edge?

I want to conclude with a lesson about the history of the official's striped shirt. Why do they wear black and white? Because there is no gray. Those shirts are black and white for a reason. The concept is an official can't be in the middle. Officials wear black and white for a symbolic reason. Those stripes are a contrast. The call is here or it is here. Officials have to take a stand or they are certain to fall, and no one wants to fall on national television in a jam-packed stadium. I know I certainly didn't.

What's the Call?

During an extra-point try, Team A fumbles at the one-yard line. Team B recovers in the end zone and attempts to run it out. Team B fumbles and Team A recovers in Team B's end zone. What is the ruling?

A. Try is ruled no good because Team B gained possession in its own end zone.

B. Award Team A one point because the fumble put the ball in the end zone.

C. Award Team A two points.

(See page 196 for answer.)

CHAPTER SEVEN:
THE BIG 12

"The man who complains about the way the ball bounces is likely the one who dropped it."

—Lou Holtz, former head coach,
University of Notre Dame

THE BIG 12 was up and running as a league before I was up and running as a Big 12 official. The Southwest Conference was going away. I didn't earn a bowl game in my final season as an SWC official, so I took that as an indicator that I hadn't had a good year.

Officially speaking, prior to the 1996 season, we officials were all out of a job. We were aware that the Big 12 was being formed and that four SWC schools were going to join the Big Eight schools to form the new conference. Using that math, I reckoned that about a third of the football officials would come from the SWC. After the season wrapped up and we had all sat around for a few months, some SWC officials started receiving phone calls from the Big 12.

My phone, however, remained eerily silent. My good friend, Richard Whittenburg, received a call, and he told me the Big 12 planned to bring me in as well. Still no call, though. One day, not too much later, my phone rang, and it was Mike Pereira, the supervisor of officials from the Western Athletic Conference.

"We know you've been working Division I football games, and we'd like you to come to work in our league," he said.

I still had not heard from the Big 12 and really began wondering if I was going to be picked to work in that league. All of a sudden, I had an offer from someone in another league who wanted me to work and be a part of a seasoned, talented crew. The WAC has a great card it can play because it's a super travel league. Mike told me, in that conference, I would have been guaranteed a game in Hawaii every year.

The offer made me feel pretty good at a point when I wasn't feeling that way at all about myself or my skills. Mike was a very nice guy and a solid official in his own right. I asked him if I could think about his offer for a couple of days. He advised me not to take too long, as he could fill the position with one phone call. He was right about that.

I wanted to talk it over with my family. This was a real dilemma. I had not heard from the Big 12, the league where I wanted to work, but I had been invited to be a part of the WAC, a league with which I had no history.

I called Richard for advice. His counsel was short and sweet.

"Don't take it," he said. "The Big 12 is going to call you."

"I don't know about that," I replied.

As it turned out, he knew something I didn't know. In the next couple of days, I didn't hear a word from the Big 12. Mike called back and asked if I had made a decision about the WAC.

"I've made up my mind," I said. "I'll come work for you."

He went through the whole routine with me, and I was excited about it. Someone wanted me in a Division I football league, and that meant a lot. The WAC was and is a good league.

The next day, my phone rang, and it was Tim Millis saying that they needed me as an official in the Big 12. I explained my situation about having given my word to the WAC. He knew about that because he and Mike were friends, but he was adamant about my coming to the Big 12.

I wondered why they were just now calling. A number of other former SWC officials already had received word. What the heck took so long? Tim explained that my name had been on the new league's list for a long time. Now I was in a difficult situation.

I had told someone I would do something, and my philosophy is once you've given someone your word, you honor your commitment. I needed another day or so to think this through. I had opportunities to work in two leagues, but I always try to do what I say I'm going to do. I stewed about it for a few days. Finally, I called Texas Tech head coach Spike Dykes and asked if I could drop by.

Spike had been instrumental in helping me become an SWC official in the first place. I have great admiration for him and consider him a great friend. I told him I had accepted a job in the Western Athletic Conference, but my heart told me that the Big 12 was a better opportunity. I knew most of the guys from the Southwest Conference, and I knew a few of the Big Eight guys. I knew very few WAC officials. I just didn't think the WAC was as good a league as the Big 12 was, no offense. I appreciated the league was willing to give me an opportunity.

Spike listened to my quandary. Then he told me how recruiting worked as the Tech head coach. He said the Raiders recruited against tough schools for the top players in the state. Many times a player would not hear from one of those other schools. Maybe the player had his heart set on Texas, but along came Texas Tech with a Division I college football scholarship. The player jumped at the chance . . . until Texas didn't get a player it wanted and came back and offered the soon-to-be-former Tech recruit a scholarship.

The player would find himself torn between his dream and his word. Spike said he always told those players to go where they would be happiest. He was not interested in anyone attending Tech with less than full enthusiasm. He wanted players to be fully committed and fully happy to be Red Raiders because other players were always available. He finished by saying my situation sounded a lot like this.

Spike never told me what to do. He just told me that story. I left and thought to myself, "Why go somewhere if your heart is somewhere else?" That cinched my decision. I called Tim Millis and said I was coming to the Big 12. I told him I was about to call the WAC and knew Mike Pereira wouldn't be happy about my choice. Tim was an NFL official at the time, and he told me Mike had just that day found out he was about to become an NFL official. Tim said to call Mike right away because it wouldn't be that bad. I called Mike, who has gone on to become the NFL supervisor of officials, and told him the Big 12 was a better fit for me. He said OK, and then made one call to Mike Wetzel, a close friend with whom I had worked on my last crew in the SWC, and filled his spot in the WAC just like that. I later heard the WAC was not happy about my choice, but I know I made the right decision.

As an official in a new league, I was convinced I needed to prove myself all over again, and I knew that would be even tougher this time around. Before that first Big 12 season, Tim told us we would be graded on every play of every game. We would see all of our work on tape each week. Good calls. Bad calls. Everything.

I worked harder than ever to become a good official when I got to the Big 12, and with Tim's guidance, we all became better officials. Within a mere three years, our league was light years ahead of other conferences in officiating because Tim worked hard to show us what he wanted, grading us over and over, explaining where we needed to be in certain situations, praising here, critiquing there. If we made a great call, he told us so. If we blew one, he shellacked us. All of it was done towards the goal of improving the quality of officiating in our league. Every grading tape ended with Tim saying something like, "You made mistakes. This crew is better than you showed in this game tape, and I will continue to expect more out of you. See you down the road."

Because of his NFL experience, Tim knew what he was doing. The level of scrutiny and the intensity of the grading were implemented from day one and came straight from the NFL. It was something to watch and something else to be a part of. The football world saw the results of better-officiated games, but on the inside we saw men who were good officials become great officials. Everyone got better, and it was fun.

Sure, the process weeded out some guys. No one was fired in the Southwest Conference, but Tim made a point of telling us early on that no Big 12 official would receive a free ride because of who he was. As it turned out, Tim fired a longtime SWC official and a close friend of his after the very first Big 12 game of the season, and unfortunately, he became an early example to the rest of us.

Either we made it in the Big 12 or we were gone. Sink or swim. Tim had pools of officials in Texas, Oklahoma, and all across the Midwest to call on. We all knew we could be replaced, literally, overnight, so we worked hard to improve. A lot of guys didn't make it from that initial group. We had some guys with a bit of age on them from each of the old leagues, and a lot of guys like me who came into the Big 12 had to retool their game.

It was difficult in the Big 12 those first few years. Everything you did was examined under a microscope, and everyone got hammered when they made mistakes. Some guys' egos couldn't take it. Tim continually amazed us with the officiating talent he brought into the league. Many of them were great officials, and they went straight to the NFL. The Big 12 not only created a larger talent pool to draw from, but it also improved the caliber of officiating.

The difference was night and day compared to the old Southwest Conference. Nothing against those guys. We had a lot of great officials in the SWC, too, but this was a brave new world when we stepped out to officiate Big 12 games in those first three years of the league. We needed to have our hats on tight and our A games in place because if we didn't, we might not be there the next Saturday. Occasionally, an official would find himself benched one game for making bad calls. It never happened to me, but I can assure you my commitment to officiating became incredibly intense beginning with the inaugural Big 12 season.

That's the small picture. From a more global perspective, the way the Big 12 came about was interesting to watch, especially for people in Texas who had an affiliation with the former Southwest Conference schools. That's because it was common knowledge that only four SWC schools were going to become part of the new league. The mystery was which four. Look at the four ultimately invited. Two (Texas and Texas A&M) had the largest enrollments, one was a state school (Tech), and one was a private school with strong political connections (Baylor, whose alumna, the late Ann Richards, was governor of Texas at the time).

A lot of controversy erupted over who made the cut, and that was interesting to observe as an official. Once it all shook out, it became a matter of blending two distinct cultures. The officials came together for our first summer meeting at a Kansas City hotel. It was great getting to know the guys from the Big Eight. They were as excited about the transition as we were. Of course, we had a little bit of the north-versus-south mentality, even among officials, and we had Big Eight aura and Southwest Conference aura, but that was to be expected under the circumstances. All of that vanished quickly in the new system.

More officials in that room had a Big Eight pedigree than had a Southwest Conference background, but the supervisor of officials was a former SWC guy, and the first Big 12 commissioner was Steve Hatchell, a former SWC commissioner. Steve deserves a lot of credit for making sure the Big 12 got its due nationally. He worked tirelessly to promote the league and increase its visibility in terms of television contracts and other promotional ties. Another important player in those early days was Donnie Duncan, director of football operations for the conference and former athletic director at Oklahoma.

Tim Millis, meanwhile, made it clear early on that this was a new conference with a lot of what many people considered superpower football schools. We had a fistful of teams with incredibly successful football histories like Oklahoma, Nebraska, and Texas. Tim told us in no uncertain terms that this was a big-time football conference, and a lot was expected from the officials in a league like this. It took only a couple of years, but Tim's visionary leadership in terms of training and scrutiny demonstrated the Big 12's officiating program was head and shoulders above those of the other major conferences. I don't say that to belittle the other leagues. We spent a lot of time watching film, and we watched film more times than not on incorrect mechanics. We spent time learning not only what to do, but why it was done.

For example, when watching film we saw a lot of the deep guys in other leagues getting beat. Receivers were getting behind them on a play, and that shouldn't happen. The deep guys—the field judge, side judge, and back judge—are taught never to let a receiver get behind them. They start seventeen yards deep, and if it's a pass play, they back up at the snap and make sure they keep the play in front of them. They can officiate while moving backward. If an official is on the sideline, he can look at the line and still keep it all in front of him, even to the point where an official goes to the pylon and stops before officiating from the goal line back toward the play.

Deep officials in the Big 12 were diligent about that specific mechanic. Realize, though, that everyone will get beat. It's going to happen because we're on the field with guys who are faster and more athletic than anyone can imagine. We used the films to learn from worst-case scenarios. An official had a receiver beat him deep and suddenly the play is on top of him. That's the worst thing that can happen to deep guys—have a play wind up in their laps where they are too close to officiate it. We're taught to move and stay out of the way because it's hard to officiate a play that falls in your lap. By keeping a buffer between oneself and the play, an official spends a lot less time fearing for his life while maintaining a better angle.

In film from other conferences, we saw officials get beat deep and work hard to officiate correctly. Then we watched NFL tapes. We rarely saw an NFL deep official get beat. They always kept the play in front of them. My impression was if an NFL official got beat deep once or twice, he probably wouldn't be there long.

Something else about the Big 12 is we used cross-field mechanics to ensure the correct spot of the ball. We talked about that in the SWC, but we didn't work at it like we had to in the Big 12 because it was a standard NFL mechanic.

Any forward progress behind the line of scrimmage was the line judge's call. It did not matter where the forward progress occurred from the line of scrimmage back; it was the line judge's responsibility. Those calls aren't as critical because it is impossible to earn a first down being tackled behind the line of scrimmage, unless there's a penalty on the defense. The mechanics called for the line judge, when he read pass, to take an easy step into the backfield and watch the tackle. If the quarterback scrambles, the line judge has to get back to the line of scrimmage because it's his call to determine whether or not a pass is thrown from behind the line. He has to know if the ball crosses the line of scrimmage and also whether or not if it was tipped before crossing, after crossing, or at the line.

That's one of those calls fans love to second-guess. The key is that the quarterback has to release the ball behind the line of scrimmage.

Many times, his arm is in motion after he crosses the line, but the ball is already out of his hand. In all of these examples, mechanics are the key to good officiating. We have to have good judgment, or we wouldn't be there, but mechanically is how we improve at that level. When I say that, I mean going through an entire game and not making a mechanical mistake. We might go through and not get every judgment right; that happens. But we should be able to go through an entire game without any mechanical mistakes. When we make mechanical mistakes, it opens us up to having our judgments second-guessed.

Yes, you have to study and know the rules, and you have to work hard at improving in those scrimmages and games, but mechanics separate the Division I guy from high school or lower-level college officials. I figured out during my Big 12 career that the league could bring in fifty-five or sixty officials, and they would all be very good. However, every organization I've ever been involved in, whatever the level of experience of the people involved, had some who were stronger than others. That is the way it is with college football officials; some are stronger.

The ones who are not as strong improve by working with the ones who are. If they don't improve, they don't last very long. The Big 12's philosophy was simple: Get better or get out. That allowed the league to introduce new guys to the process and start over. We tried to help the new guys. I think we have to be unselfish about teaching officiating because no one gets there alone. We might have a new guy on our crew or maybe have a guy on our crew who is just having a hard time. We knew he didn't receive good ratings the year before, and now he's part of our crew. The league made a couple of changes each year. We're out there on a Saturday afternoon, and one guy can make everyone look bad. That's why we spent a lot of time helping each other.

Speaking of help, we received plenty from Big 12 coaches. During the off season, they loved talking to us and getting to know us, but when a game started, it's like we suddenly turned into the ultimate evildoers. The love was over, and we were the outcasts. I've always thought that was interesting. When we're on the sideline before a game, everyone wants to talk to us and shake our hands, but once the ball is kicked off, you can go ahead and paint the bull's-eye on our backs.

Something else we came to understand about the Big 12 was that League Commissioner Steve Hatchell went out and procured lucrative television contracts. The Big 12 had six or seven of its schools on television every week in one of the biggest college football deals at the time. That was one of the reasons for the SWC's demise—not enough television. This new league had a new audience, and the pressure was on to deliver a quality product, which included quality officiating. The Big 12 made no bones about it. We were told that we could mess up the league by not providing quality officiating, which would result in bad games. Conversely, we could help make the league better by becoming officials of the highest quality. We hadn't reached that standard by day one or even by the end of the first season, though.

I think people realized the Big 12 was a great training ground. We had a current NFL official as our supervisor, and he was adamant about our using many of their mechanics. I worked with at least a dozen guys who went on to the NFL during the first few years of the Big 12. They were mostly young guys who could give the NFL a lot of years. After a while it became fairly obvious that a number of other conferences were using our mechanics, and when we watched film from those leagues, we saw their mistakes and identified how and why they made them.

All this is the real difference between the levels of officiating from conference to conference. It had its impact elsewhere in college football. In the current bowl system (the BCS), officials from the major conferences rotate and get one BCS game each year, depending on where that particular league's teams wind up, because of the need for neutral crews. After that, you take the next tier of bowls, which are really good games, too, and one of those might be the big game for officials from, say, Conference USA, a league outside of the BCS.

We would watch some of those games because often a Big 12 school was competing in them. I remember the 2003 Alamo Bowl between Nebraska and Michigan State, which had a crew from one of the non–BCS leagues officiating. It was a big game, a close game eventually won by Nebraska, and those guys weren't used to working with that caliber of teams with that kind of crowd and that kind of pressure. Officials notice which conference's crew has been assigned to a particular bowl game, and it shows up in the officiating. Those non–BCS crews are not used to the speed of players from Oklahoma and Florida, for example. It's a big environment with a huge vocal crowd and savvy coaches on the sidelines who understand how to work officials. That crew might think it's just a football game, but it's not. It's a different world from working in a non–BCS league every week. That's just the way it is.

When we officiate at that level week after week, season after season, we become accustomed to those things. Take a crew from a smaller conference and put them on the field with Nebraska, and that's a big deal to them, maybe even a high-water mark of their career. For us, it's a weekly deal. Look at NBA officials. Guys who work at that level work it every night. Someone who's not been in that situation regularly would likely find the game too fast for them.

Every league is different in terms of finding its own officiating identity, and we struggled with that a little during the early years of the Big 12 with what we would call in certain situations and how we would call it. Tim, to his credit, spent part of the offseason visiting each member school's coach and gathering their input (read: complaints) on officiating. He would then counter that by explaining our philosophy and would back us every time he could. Coaches didn't agree many times, but Tim had such a great working knowledge of the game and how a game should be officiated that they all respected him.

During the season, it was a different story. Coaches called him, and some perceived controversy came up every week. Tim would receive at least one tape each week from a coach urging him to look at something because "his guys didn't do a good job." Sometimes Tim would disagree with the coach and say we were right and why. Sometimes he didn't. Teams had their own reasons for sending the tapes in.

Here's an example: One year, Kansas State played a non-conference opponent who ran an offense that featured a play that included a chop block of a defensive player in the middle of the line. The block was virtually impossible for the wing official to see. It was obviously a coached technique in which the player was taught to complete this blatantly illegal move. It happened at least five times in that game, and K-State head coach Bill Snyder sent a tape to the conference office showing these plays which included at least one instance in which his player was injured. Unfortunately, the Big 12 crew working that game missed those calls, and to my knowledge, no action was taken against the offending school.

Sending tapes to the conference office is just one way coaches like to wield their influence, whether they are on or off the field. Of course, I have seen subtle and not-so-subtle examples of this, as well, over the years.

For example, Terry Allen was the new head coach at Kansas in 1997, and the Jayhawks were home to a highly rated Nebraska team. With a few minutes to go before halftime, a bank of lights went out on the Kansas side. Our crew stopped the clock and talked it over. We decided to get the coaches and discuss the situation in the middle of the field. I went over to get Nebraska head coach Tom Osborne and gave him a heads-up about what was going to happen. He said he'd been to a number of high school games where they didn't have as many lights as we still had. I thought to myself, *Our decision has just been made*. He was the dean of coaches. We had a fairly new referee and Allen, the new coach at Kansas.

Osborne encouraged us to play on, so that's what we did. In the early days of the league, Tom was quite an influence. If he had input about officiating in the conference, it was generally heard. One of the highlights of my career was working the sideline in front of Tom's great Nebraska teams.

The important thing to remember is that we were getting the calls right. I'm not saying we didn't have controversies, but they have those in every league—critical calls someone can point to and say they might have had an effect on the outcome of the game. We could tell by the "ding" tapes that guys were getting the calls right, and many of the more seasoned guys were not showing up in the tapes much. They knew what the league wanted to be called, and how the league wanted them called, so in case we didn't see something or just looked the wrong way at the wrong time, getting "dinged" on the tape was pretty rare after the first three or four years of the league.

Now, new guys were getting "dinged," but that's the way the system operated. It was designed to make them improve. They told us it was all about constructive criticism, but I've never seen that in anything else I've ever been involved with. Guys were getting better, though. You could see their confidence growing. I was fortunate to have been on great crews with officials who had been around a while throughout my Big 12 career. We had a lot of confidence and didn't get "dinged" very often. The league expected us to be good, and so did we.

Despite the pressure, the job was fun, and much of that was because of the personalities I encountered through the years on the sideline. I've talked about Spike Dykes at Texas Tech and the influence he's had on me, and I've also mentioned Bob Stoops and the tremendous respect I have for his abilities in restoring Oklahoma to national prominence. And there were others such as Les Miles, who did a great job at Oklahoma State before taking the LSU job, and Rick Neuheisel, the outstanding coach at Colorado who took the UCLA job recently. Another guy I admire, although he wasn't a Big 12 coach, is Jimmie Keeling, who led Lubbock Estacado to a state championship at the high school level and later became head coach at Hardin-Simmons University in Abilene, Texas, where he brought prominence to a program that had not competed in football for almost forty years.

Former Iowa State coach Dan McCarney is a coach who officials genuinely enjoyed working with. He might not have won a national championship or many bowl games, but he worked hard, loved his players, and treated officials with the utmost respect. He enjoyed some success, but he was playing in a tough league with a short stick. I would bet 95 percent of the officials in the Big 12 would tell you he was the best-liked coach in the league when he was there.

Of course, sooner or later, every official finds someone he doesn't like or has a run-in with a coach he can't quite put behind him. That includes me, by the way. It's hard to put it behind you when someone treats you poorly as a person. It is too bad they all can't be like Coach McCarney. He is the kind of guy you want your son playing for, and that's not to say the other coaches in the league weren't.

I also liked working at Texas A&M with head coach R.C. Slocum. He was a real gentleman and a great coach and another coach who treated officials with the utmost respect. One of the most enjoyable aspects of being a line judge is bringing the home team out of the locker room before the game and at halftime. Many times I would enter a dressing room with the field judge, and he would leave with the team captains. I've had a chance to hear coaches give those final talks, and I've always enjoyed going in there and listening to them. Many times, the coach will run everyone else out of the dressing room because there's always some media, school officials, and boosters hanging around. Bob Stoops at Oklahoma and Bobby Bowden at Florida State were two I know of who ran everyone out so they could have the final word.

At the end of the day, coaches such as Tom Osborne, Bobby Bowden, and Bob Stoops are motivators, the CEOs of their organizations. The ultimate responsibility falls to them. I notice those head coaches on the sideline. They don't do a lot of coaching. Coordinators meet with their respective units, and coordinators call the plays. Position coaches handle their duties, but by and large, the head coach is an encourager and motivator. The ones who are the most successful are those CEO-type coaches who do exactly that. Guys who try to be coordinators and the CEO at the same time are generally not as successful. Football is a business, and they have to run their organizations like that. I watched these men and tried to bring back some of their tactics to my job as CEO of City Bank Texas.

It was a great thrill to have worked Coach Bowden's sideline in two bowl games and once at home against Colorado. However, my fondest memory was when this Coach Bowden came to Lubbock to speak at a Fellowship of Christian Athletes banquet sponsored by City Bank Texas. He held a news conference at the bank. It was the week that all the speculation was going on around the country and in Lubbock that Bob Knight might be coming to Texas Tech as the new head basketball coach. One of the media members asked Coach Bowden, "What do you think about Bob Knight?"

Coach Bowden thought a few seconds and said, "I think he is a disciplinarian. There aren't many of us left!"

You can tell a coach who is organized and has his stuff together. The level doesn't matter. I've seen them from the smallest class of high schools to Division I. Those are coaches who don't get penalties for not having enough (or too many) men on the field. It's a business. I saw a lot more of that in the Big 12 than I did in the SWC.

I guess the biggest difference, to me, was the Southwest Conference was sort of a family-run business. You had people who had done things their own way for a long time and been successful . . . right up until the day they weren't successful anymore. The Big 12, on the other hand, was corporate America. It was all business. Nothing personal. And that's all right, too.

What's the Call?

Team A punts the ball. Team B's deep receiver touches the ball at the five, and it rolls into his own end zone. The deep receiver then picks up the ball and attempts to run it out of the end zone but is tackled by Team A in the end zone. What is the ruling?

A. Touchback, Team B ball first and ten at the twenty

B. Safety, award Team A two points

C. Team A rekicks from previous stop

(See page 196 for answer.)

CHAPTER EIGHT:
A LOVE OF THE GAME

"Anyone who robs Peter to pay Paul can always depend upon Paul's vote."

—Will Rogers

*" THE TEST RESULTS ARE IN,
WE'VE RULED OUT ANYTHING CHEAP. "*

ONE OF THE most common misconceptions I confronted as a college official is the notion that we are highly compensated. "You guys must have raked in a bundle to officiate that big game," a fan would say, but nothing could have been further from the truth. Two decades ago, when I was a line judge for the Southwest Conference, I earned only $400 per game. In 2005, my last season, I earned $1,000 per game for my work as a Big 12 Conference official. I am not privy to the numbers, but one would be hard pressed to believe college football revenues haven't increased significantly since then. Conferences have signed megadeals with television networks, and more games than ever are on TV each week. On top of that, imagine the revenues from parking, concessions, and merchandise and stadium suites, not to mention the volume of ticket sales. Obviously, these revenue streams fall under the purview of individual universities, but regardless, it's amazing how much money is generated at a college football game and how little of it is used to compensate those officials who perform a vital function at each one of those games.

Sadly, the trend has always been to treat compensation for officials as an afterthought. At the same time, though, the demand is for excellence beyond compare. Looking at it from that standpoint, it seems justifiable that the premier conferences should reevaluate and provide their officials more in the way of compensation. It just makes sense. I served as CEO of City Bank Texas for more than twenty years. This is an exemplary corporation of more than 700 employees experiencing substantial success and growth. I have an understanding of what it takes to achieve excellence. I understand the motivating factors which drive people not only to work, but to be the best they can be. I expect excellence in the corporate setting and compensate my employees accordingly. Shouldn't football conferences reaping millions of dollars in television revenue put the same standards in place?

I quit officiating on the field when I was fifty-eight, even though I probably had another season or two left in me. I was fortunate enough that I didn't have to do it for the money. I know seasoned football officials are out there right now weighing the wear and tear of travel and saying to themselves that it's not as much fun anymore. Frankly, I shared those same thoughts. However, if those officials were being compensated properly, the conferences would likely get more mileage out of them. The worth of a practiced and wise official is greatly undervalued. As it is, the system takes advantage of officials.

When I first started with the SWC, I was given a game check and a little bit of pay for travel. The league had a set amount it would pay, depending on whether an official was going to Houston from Lubbock or to Dallas or College Station or Austin. The Southwest Conference also offered its officials a $35 per diem for a maximum of two days. This system led to two and sometimes three of us rooming together in hotels. I was traveling from Lubbock, so most of the time I received a game fee, per diem, and travel. It totaled about $1,000. I was flying Southwest Airlines, which was not expensive, staying at inexpensive hotels, and eating pretty average food. Prior to that, though, I was working high school games and receiving minimal compensation for travel and a small game fee.

Getting a $1,000 check from the conference in 1988 to work a football game was a big deal to me. However, compared to the amount the league was making at that time and certainly looking at how much revenue it generates today, the compensation of officials is one of the large inequities in college football. It's a paradox brought on, to some extent, by officials themselves.

Any official working high school or small college football games today who gets a call from a major conference to work in that particular league is going to pay attention. If the Southwest Conference had called me when I was just starting out in Morton, Texas, and asked me to work SWC games without pay, I would have jumped at the chance. I'm sure 99 percent of the officials I've known would have taken that deal, because it's an opportunity to do something that's considered to be priceless. I never asked how much I was going to be paid because I didn't care. I think it's a given in officiating circles that we are not going to make much money. At least, that's the way most officials look at it. The Southwest Conference could have lined up fifty-one or fifty-two guys and had them officiate all of their games for free. No college football official is in it for the money. We do it for the love of the game.

Officials are not naïve, though. Most of us are fairly savvy businessmen, and most of us were able to get to that level of officiating because we've had some success in other parts of our lives. We have officials representing a broad spectrum of professions, and they all know they are getting the short end of the financial stick. Imagine a nationally televised sellout at Texas or Texas A&M. Major bucks are being brought in by the conference. Consider those seven seasoned officials in their individual crucial roles, individuals without whom the game could not be fairly played. Yet the conference is paying a mere $7,000 for a highly trained crew that is critical to the continued success of the game.

The problem is that there is little the officials can do to improve their situation. We know that if one of us refused to work for this pay, the league would say fine and pick from a thousand others lined up for that spot. Conferences take advantage of that.

Another aspect of the financial and logistical difficulties encountered by football officials is travel. I quickly discovered that getting to the Big 12 campuses was a more costly undertaking than it was in the Southwest Conference. Big 12 officials were working more pressurized games under more scrutiny than ever. This was a bigger league that required more travel. In officiating, the conference dictates what will be paid based on the distance from his home to the game destination. From Lubbock, I was paid so many cents per mile from my home to wherever I happened to be working that Saturday. I drove to the Lubbock airport, paid for parking, purchased an airline ticket, and flew to the game site.

Traveling on Fridays to and from a college town is always a challenge just because of the large number of college students trying to get to where they're going. It boils down to officials making reservations well in advance and then crossing their fingers and hoping the flights work out. I remember trying to get to the Texas Tech–Texas game in 1989. It was a big game for both schools. Tech hadn't defeated Texas in Austin in twenty-two years. Spike Dykes had been a Longhorn assistant coach for years before becoming Tech's head coach. Couple that with the fact that David McWilliams, then the head coach at UT, had left Tech after one season (1986) to return to Austin. It looked like the perfect storm, and the fans were all coming to watch. I planned to fly to Austin from Lubbock with a stopover in Dallas, so I drove to Lubbock from Morton on a Friday afternoon and got on a plane loaded with Tech fans bound for Austin. Since I was from the area, people knew who I was and why I was on the plane. When we reached Dallas, the weather turned bad and we were delayed there until nearly midnight. Finally, the plane, loaded with the Red Raider faithful and me, took off for Austin. The delay caused me to miss the Friday night pregame, throwing my routine out of whack.

In the Big 12, virtually any trip to the North Division required a flight to Kansas City, where our crew would meet, rent a car, and drive to our destination. For instance, travel from Lubbock to Columbia, Missouri, for a Missouri Tigers game, was a three-day event. Friday is the travel day. Saturday is the work day, and Sunday is the return day. Another tangle in the travel web is the fact that few of the college towns in the Big 12 had direct airline service from a major carrier. The fee of the connecting smaller airlines was simply unaffordable on our budget.

An official might receive travel expenses of $300 or so and would be paid a per diem of between $50 and $65. The league would pay a two-day maximum. Depending on where he lived, an official might receive a check for between $1,300 and $1,500 for salary, travel, and per diem. Commonly, the travel reimbursement and per diem did not cover all of the expenses associated with the trip, which meant the official had to cover the balance of his expenses from his game fee.

The Big 12 had a couple of options for booking hotel rooms. Officials could make their own reservations or the league could reserve rooms for them. It's still the same way today. It's not a glamorous deal, and we didn't have valets or our own entourages paving the way for us and taking care of the details. Whether the home football weekend was in Waco, Texas, home of the Baylor Bears, or Manhattan, Kansas, home of the Kansas State Wildcats, it was the same: a weekend set aside for football. Every hotel in town had a set rate for that weekend, and the hotels did not reduce that rate for any reason. They knew another customer would happily take a room someone else didn't want, regardless of price. There were no breaks on room rates for game officials.

Typically, our hotel arrangements would be made by the secretary to the supervisor of officials. She was responsible for trying to find a hotel near the game site and blocking four rooms for Friday and Saturday nights. Another factor in the booking equation was dealing with certain officials' personalities. Some preferred a room by themselves; others would want four guys in a room so they wouldn't have to pay as much. The league would block the rooms for two nights, but if we were able to leave Saturday, we did. Officials, just like anyone else, were in no mood to spend one more night at a game site if they had a flight out of Kansas City bright and early the next morning. Most hotels required a two-day minimum. Many times not only did we pay the hotel at the game site for two nights, we'd ante up for a hotel room to be closer to the airport for an early morning departure. Those later flights were often destined for delays, which equated to more time away from our families. Taxis, rental cars, parking, meals, gratuities, it all adds up.

Imagine the excitement of the game day crowd with throngs of people surging toward the stadium early and traffic backed up for miles and sometimes for hours. Those traffic issues can wreak havoc for the officiating crew trying to arrive early for their game day preparations. If you've ever been to an Oklahoma Sooners game, you know that on game day the traffic travels at the speed of a turtle once you turn off I-35 headed east to the stadium. Arriving four hours before kickoff was the only way we could ensure ourselves a timely start to our preparations.

Not all of the game sites were problematic, though. For instance, Texas A&M has a hotel in the student center directly across from Kyle Field. That hotel was one of the best venues for us because the only people who stayed there were the Aggies' most generous boosters and game officials. All we had to do was walk from the hotel to the stadium, which made for a great situation. For Texas Tech games in Lubbock, the officials are transported from a hotel near the stadium in a van with a police escort. This allows the officials to focus on the game rather than any distraction caused by accommodations, traffic, or transportation. Leaving the game for the postgame meeting is easier, as well. By comparison, Austin is tougher. Hotels are farther away from the stadium. We fight traffic getting in and out just like the rest of the crowd.

Not surprisingly, part of our crew's pregame always included spending some time talking about the next week's travel arrangements. We sat down and talked about who was getting the car, who was arriving when, who was riding with whom, and all the monkey wrenches that could be thrown in there through plane delays, mechanical problems, or weather. The average person might not realize the logistics involved in bringing seven or eight guys from different parts of the country to one of those Big 12 schools on a Friday afternoon, and every game was different. As four or five of us arrived at Kansas City International Airport on Friday afternoon, one or two would grab the rental car and then return to the airport to wait for the others before making the drive to one of the North Division game sites. Imagine our dilemma whenever someone was delayed for a couple of hours or more. The guys would head to the Friday night pregame meeting. The delayed official had to finagle another rental car (if available) and arrive late into the night only to arise early for the game the following day.

The sacrifice on the part of the individual official suddenly becomes apparent when the true details are even superficially examined. All this for three hours on the field, for the love of the game? Any regular business traveler understands these kinds of sacrifices happen on a regular basis; the difference for officials is we're traveling on weekends to college destinations that thousands of others also are trying to reach.

No one ever said life was fair, but what about an equitable solution to these challenges? The next thing that needs to happen in officiating is that salaries need to be commensurate with the job. Coaches, players, and fans expect the best. The system in place today requires top-tier performance at bargain-basement salaries. The conference should pay more, expect the best, and get the best. Every official in the league knows the major conferences have significant television contracts, at least one guaranteed spot in the Bowl Championship Series, and other bowl tie-ins. The leagues are bringing in, literally, millions, and officials are not even being paid peanuts.

What if, for instance, an official made $3,000 a week and had his travel paid? He could be required to spend six hours of his work week studying, with a mandatory test that becomes part of his weekly preparation routine. Officials would spend more time during the season studying and preparing. I know the weeks that I spent five or six hours in preparation resulted in better game performances for me, my crew, the teams, and ultimately the conference. I am the first to admit that I didn't always do as good of a job of preparing as I could have. However, if we want better officiating, perhaps the lesson could be taken from the corporate world. Expect quality and pay accordingly.

I think eventually there will be a national pool of football officials. In basketball, there are officials who work games in two or three leagues. It is a large pool of officials. In the NFL, crews are made up of officials all across the country, and a crew may be sent anywhere in the nation.

In the college game, with a national pool, the same crew might work at Florida State one week and Oregon State the next. That will cost more in travel, and it may or may not be a solution to the pay problem. Today several conferences are working together to make up crews of officials from across the conferences. Those crews would work all games in all of those conferences. This might work if all these conferences were BCS and major football conferences, but that is not the case.

The primary goal of the conference should be that each seven-man officiating crew works together as one cohesive unit and gets every call right. Personally, I wanted to be the best college official I could be and to improve every game. I wanted to be with officials who were of a similar mind, with other guys who also wanted to improve. I had no desire to become an NFL official. I made good money in my regular job, and I loved college football. One of my primary goals each season was to officiate the league championship game. This was where the top-rated official at each position landed at the end of the season. Alternatively, a chance to work in a BCS bowl game or one of the other bowls assigned to our conference marked the end of a season well done. And the rewards should follow: a quality schedule for the next season and the right pay.

Improved pay isn't a cure-all solution, but if conferences were willing to pay more money in game fees, travel, and to provide assistance financially in prep time and training, they would reap the benefits. Right now, conferences believe that if an official is not willing to work in the current system, they can find someone who will. That ever-growing pool of officials is something a lot of people want to be part of, but no one ever came into Division I college football as the ultimate official.

An official starts relearning the game the minute he steps on the field with two Division I football teams. No matter how good an official is, he's not good enough the first time he's on the field with Colorado and Nebraska. Officials have the tools and the ability and know the rules. They have great talent, reactions, speed, and agility, but until an official knows how to react in a Division I game with proper mechanics, it is a different game. They have to know where they are going on the field before they get there. I started officiating in Division I at age forty. I retired eighteen years later. Never could I beat a D-1A player running on the field any time in my career. I had to understand the mechanics and move to the next position before they got there. This is a skill which is taught in a mechanics book, and film sessions but can't be aptly applied without game experience.

When the ball was snapped on the five-yard line, I, as a line judge, moved to the goal line and officiated back because I knew I couldn't beat the players to the goal if I waited at the line of scrimmage. It was the same case for a back judge if he saw a pass play developing. If his key was the tight end, and the tight end was blocking, the back judge wasn't in such a hurry to get back. He would go to his secondary read and look at the next key. If he saw it as a running play, he would stay and watch the blocking. A Division I football player can chew up fifteen yards pretty quickly, so a back judge had better be able to move backwards in a hurry and never let anyone get behind him if he reads pass.

College football officials will never be defined by the money they make. They're barely able to cover expenses. I am reminded of Bobby Jones, the amateur golfer who played the sport purely for the love of the game. In the 1940s and 1950s, there were a number of great amateur golfers who did not want to become pros. College athletes are the last of the great amateurs, and officials are a large part of that equation. The great majority of officials do it simply because they love the sport.

Something worth understanding about officials is that we are not employees of the conferences; we are independent contractors. Conferences go to great lengths to specify this in contractual language. No insurance, no workers comp, no employer/employee relationship. Generally, a conference will tell its officials, "Here is the deal. Play by our rules or we will find someone who will." Officials are not sought after for their political views or corporate philosophies. They are to make sure a contest is played fairly between the lines on the field.

What was one of the primary purposes of college institutions coming together to form a conference? Some people might say it was a result of geography. Teams had to travel long distances and officials from the local area were used to call the games. Sometimes the officiating was less than fair. One of the primary goals of forming these leagues was to provide competent, neutral officiating for all sports in that league. Today leagues have expanded roles to include negotiating TV contracts, bowl games, and all the modern functions into which the current conferences have evolved.

In the premier conferences, football drives the bus. Basketball is strong, make no mistake, but in those first, crucial, formative years, football gave the Big 12 its identity. As a producer of revenue, football takes the front seat. Truly, it's an honor to be chosen to officiate Big 12 football.

"Why?" you ask.

I hope I've made that clear.

For the love of the game.

What's the Call?

A defensive back for Team B is defending against a legal forward pass beyond the neutral zone. He has his back to the ball and is waving his arms in the face of an eligible Team A receiver who, in his attempt to catch the pass, makes no contact with the Team B player. The pass falls incomplete. What is the ruling?

A. No contact by Team B player, so pass is ruled incomplete.

B. Pass interference by Team B but ignore because no contact.

C. Pass interference by Team B, spot foul or fifteen yards from previous spot if less than fifteen yards.

(See page 196 for answer.)

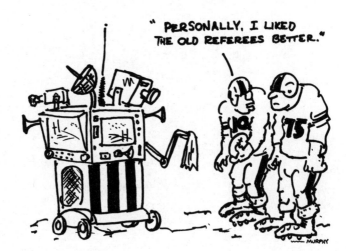

CHAPTER NINE:
CONSISTENCY IS ITS OWN REWARD

---

*"Men forget everything; women remember everything. That's why men
need instant replays in sports. They've already forgotten what happened."*

— Rita Rudner

ONE SECRET TO being a successful college football official is understanding this paradox: The game moves fast, so slow it down.
That was something my supervisors consistently said to me: Slow it
down and let the game come to you. During the first few years of my
officiating career, I thought I had to be moving when the ball was
snapped.

The reality is that officials see a lot more when they're standing still. The learned skill is an ability to slow the whole thing down in your mind and see it in slow motion. That is especially true with fumbles and receptions near the sideline or in the end zone. On a catch, for example, you have to see the foot inbounds while sensing the ball in possession, and then confirm possession of the ball.

If an official is standing on the sideline watching a receiver trying to complete a catch near the sideline, that official should always look at the receiver's feet first, and then worry about whether or not he has possession. The old saying is that the ground can't cause a fumble, but it sure can cause an incompletion, and a sequence of events like this happens in the blink of an eye. It takes a lot of repetitions to see all of that correctly in that narrow time frame, but the more times an official does it, the more snaps he sees, the more plays he has, the more the official "gets it."

One cardinal rule of officiating: Don't watch the ball. That was one of the tallest hurdles I had to overcome. Players know they have to be moving when the ball is snapped, and that's also what an official thinks the first time he lines up. Really, though, that's the last thing an official needs to be doing. Instead, the official should watch the play, read the keys, and practice what he has learned about the game. It's difficult to do after having played the game because it's a completely different perspective.

Still, it's not entirely different from the role of players. Defensive players learn to read their keys. They see the way a play is developing and react to it. Officiating is not unlike that. We have certain keys we must learn, as well. For example, the men on the wings, the head linesman and line judge, watch the snap take place after the long checklist of things they have to watch prior to the snap. Once the quarterback has the ball, he's the referee's responsibility. The wing officials see where the ball is. If it's coming their way, they focus on the blocks. If the play is going away from him, they trail it; if it's up the middle, they watch the blocking.

The best way to accomplish all of that is to stand still. It's only when the ball carrier is even with one of the guys on the wing that they move with him. That way, if he fumbles, steps out of bounds, or is face-masked, the official will see it. If it's a fumble, officials drop their bean bag to mark the spot of the end of the run in case there is a flag on the play, and that spot should become an enforcement spot. It is important here to stay off the whistle. Determine if the ball is still in bounds and who recovered it, then move in and make the call. Until a play is made on the ball carrier, we watch the blocking. It is almost like playing a zone defense. When the ball is in your zone, you react a certain way. When it's going away from you, other actions are required. Early in my career, I had to make myself stop moving when the ball was snapped and not watch the ball.

I learned to officiate high school football from watching other high school officials. That's the only way to do it. In this business, someone has to help us learn, and we have to pay attention and learn the truisms of officiating.

Truism No. 1: You cannot call everything you see. Everything isn't necessarily relevant to the play; for example, a holding infraction that occurs on the opposite side of the line of scrimmage from a running play, a player, who isn't involved in the play, has an unbuckled chinstrap. If officials called everything they saw, games would take too long and fans would believe officials were unnecessarily injecting themselves into the game. In other words, it would kill the sport's appeal. Young officials tend to look for everything they can find. They have to get over that, and that was something that took me a while.

Slowing the game down in your mind takes time and experience. When a player is being tackled, slow the play down almost frame by frame and then look for the ball. When a ball carrier moves beyond the line of scrimmage and all the blocking, the first thing the official has to sense again is the ball. He has to know it is in the player's possession without having to think about it. He has to feel it, as there are too many other things to watch, think about, and react to so as not to take concentration from the play at hand. Then it's a matter of determining whether the ball carrier is down by virtue of a body part—elbow, knee, shoulder, anything other than a foot or hand hitting the ground.

If the official believes the player still has the ball, he's 90 percent home on whether to rule if a fumble occurred or if the player was down. Every official has that laundry list of things he has to do on every single play. Each of the seven different positions on a crew has a list of responsibilities. Those are the finer points of officiating, and they are hard to teach. When an official lets the game come to him, lets the blocks come to him, that is officiating as it ought to be.

Everyone wants to talk about holding, including coaches. Division I officials understand holding better than anyone else on the field because it is drilled into them year after year, week after week, test after test, training film after training film. When the game is over, and we're submitting game reports, we can't just write in our report that at 8:23 in the first quarter No. 74 Red was holding at Team B's twenty-four yard line. As I mentioned in an earlier chapter, our reports require a verb. The minute a player jerks, pulls, restricts, hooks, or tugs, we have holding—provided it takes place at the point of attack. What young coaches and officials alike do not understand is that an offensive and defensive player can be wrapped up and "dancing" with each other, but until that defensive player makes a move to get out of the dance and the offensive player does something to try and keep that from happening holding is not going to be called at the D-1A level.

As a line judge, the conversations I had with the defensive ends and cornerbacks were always the same. "Mr. Ref, that tackle is holding me," they'd say. "He is grabbing my jersey and holding me back."

Now, as I pointed out earlier, the tackle on my side is one of my primary keys. I watch him on every play. It is something I don't have to think about. My eyes had only flickered off him for fractions of seconds when I looked to check my receiver. If there was any holding going on, I already have made up my mind whether it was restrictive enough to warrant a flag.

So I'll answer something like, "I saw him. You weren't trying to get away from him very hard. Show me something, and you might get the call."

Fumbles. Receptions. Holding. Go back and look at the controversial calls in any football game, and those three topics will cover about 80 percent of it.

Something else about becoming a good official, which is no secret, is that it requires consistency. If we are consistently good, the people who matter, such as coaches, players, and fellow officials, will notice. The highest quality officials officiate the first play of the game just like the last play and then get out of there.

At the line judge position, consistency is most noticeable when marking forward progress. This is something that occurs on each play. It does not take many plays into a game for everyone to have an opinion as to whether I am accurate or not. The observers in the press box, coaches in the press box, people at home watching the yellow line on TV (which we do not have), players, coaches on the field, and other members of the crew all have opinions about forward progress. It has to be right every time.

Consistency requires a certain temperament, which is a big part of being successful at the highest levels of officiating. Officials must be able to withstand pressure from the coaches, self-imposed pressure, and pressure from the league office to make the right call all the time. An environment like that is not suitable for everyone, but officials who control what they are doing and avoid allowing others to control them are the ones who have been properly trained and know the rules. Someone who is affected by outside pressures like angry coaches on either side of the field or who is afraid to throw a flag right in front of those same angry coaches cannot do well. It takes courage to throw the flag.

The first really big game I worked in my career was a Colorado–Texas Monday nighter at Boulder in 1989. I called a personal foul late in the game in front of the Texas bench while the Longhorns were driving. I called the penalty, and it made for some angry Longhorns. But once an official gets past that, even if he's wrong (which wasn't the case here), he still has to make the call and have the courage and temperament to accept the heat. Officials who can do that will be all right.

This business requires a thick skin, and officials receive plenty of chances to develop that rawhide. It may come in the form of public criticism from the media, but it's more likely to arrive in the form of feedback from the conference office. Hearing someone say, "This is an unacceptable call," or "You missed two offsides in a row; what were you looking at?" or "We would have supported holding on this call," requires a certain level of mental toughness.

Any official who is criticized five or six times for his performance the week before is sure to be sliding down in his chair because he and his entire crew are hearing it. Maybe it's just his week. Whatever the reason for the tough critique, an official must be able to put all of that behind him because he's about to work another game. Two bad games in a row, and that official might need to find another conference to work in. It happens. I've seen officials on the side who weren't able to put their mistakes behind them. They went out the next game and compounded things with more poor work, and then they weren't invited back the next season.

I've seen officials crash and burn. I've seen some hang around too long. I've seen officials put on a crew because the supervisor thought they could do the job, and it turned out they were marginal. People can help get officials in the conference, but they sure can't keep them in, so if they manage to hang around eighteen or twenty years, surely they're doing something right. Will officials make mistakes? You bet. We all do from time to time, even the best of us.

Take an exaggerated example like the infamous "fifth-down" controversy between Colorado and Missouri in 1990, when Colorado received five downs and scored a touchdown to win the game and preserve their undefeated record. That is a crew mistake because everyone on the crew keeps up with every down. It is the head linesman's responsibility first and foremost, but the final check is the line judge. The line judge is supposed to look at the down box over the shoulder of the head linesman after every play before the ball is snapped on the next play to make sure what's showing on the box matches the down indicator on his hand. He will also look at the scoreboard and check it, although the scoreboard isn't official. Only the down box on the head linesman's side of the field and the conference play-by-play scorer in the press box are official. If the only one that's wrong is the scoreboard, the official disregards it.

A mistake like that leads to the entire crew being disciplined, which generally results in a suspension. That is a dramatic thing. Another crew has to be brought in to work the next week and we know neither coaches nor officials like change. In a major conference, though, a good chance exists that no crew will work eleven or twelve consecutive weeks, especially if the league happens to be in head-to-head play. Usually, at least one crew is idle each week.

The league will tell the coaches a crew is being suspended, and another crew that was scheduled to be off will work that game. The new crew, which has no reservations, suddenly has to pack, cancel plans, and find a way to get to the game location on short notice. That can be both a dramatic and traumatic experience.

Now, here's the question in the minds of officials: If we've made a mistake, how does suspending us make us any better? A football team that has blown a big game one week wants to do everything it can to put that experience behind it and prove it's better than what it showed that particular day. We're the same way, but somehow supervisors of officials believe suspensions are the way to go. I've never been able to reconcile that in my mind; I cannot see how forcing someone to sit out makes that person better. Really, all that will happen is he will sit around, dwell on it, and have a sick feeling. It takes self-confidence and ego to get on that field to begin with. Take that away, and the official has lost one of the ingredients that make him what he is.

Some might argue suspensions teach officials that mistakes have immediate repercussions. However, a better approach might be to require that official to undergo additional work or testing in the offseason. Maybe the conference gives him a nine- or ten-game schedule the following season instead of eleven. That way, he continues to work with confidence this season and probably works a little harder the next season as a result of knowing he was penalized. I don't believe in having officials sit down. If that official is not good enough to work this week, he is not good enough to be in the league. The average fan believes that suspensions should happen, but why? Football is a game of mistakes. Coaches make them. Players make them. Fans make them. Media members make them.

Officials generally fall into two categories when it comes to mistakes: officials who want the play coming toward them, and those who don't. The ones who want the play coming towards them don't live in fear while they are on the field. The others, on the other hand, do. If it's fourth down and goal with the ball on the two-yard line, and the offense decides to go for it, a good official wants the play coming his way. I think great players have that attitude, too. Defensive players want the ball coming toward them; offensive players just want the ball. We're the same way. My attitude was always, "Come at me." I've officiated with guys who were just happy to be out there, and they weren't at all interested in making that tough call. They didn't want anything to threaten their career. They preferred to be one of those guys who could tell his friends he officiated college football.

We have to be able to make the tough call and understand that with the tough call comes the chance for being wrong. I can't say how many times in my career I've been in a short-yardage situation in a Nebraska–Oklahoma, Texas A&M–Texas, or a Colorado–Nebraska game. And every time, I was thinking, "Come this way. I want to see this play and make the call."

Maybe I'm wrong. I'm sure some of my fellow officials, having just read this, will disagree. But I believe every official knows in his heart if he wants the big play to come his way. Having said all that, I've clearly drawn a line between two kinds of officials. Which one do coaches, players, and fans want out there?

Another truism about officiating is that a career can end on the next play because the next play might be the one where an official isn't concentrating, and he makes a terrible call in a crucial situation. Just as important, he could be seriously injured. With instant replay today (more on this later), that is probably not going to happen. But what if an official calls a touchdown and it's not one? How many times have you ever seen a touchdown taken off the scoreboard? It didn't happen until the advent of replay.

Officials are taught that they must see the ball in the end zone. From the five-yard line in, officials on the wings (the head linesman and line judge) go to the goal line the instant the ball is snapped. "That's the money line," to quote Tim Millis. Even if the play is still developing in the backfield, officials have to be ready at the goal line because here they come. Early in my career, I was as excited as anyone to call a touchdown. The seasoned official gets to the goal line and lets the play come to him. Then he makes sure the ball is in an offensive player's possession in the end zone and acts like he's been there before, calmly raising his arms to signal touchdown. Once a player crosses the goal line, it doesn't matter if an official calls a touchdown a tenth of a second later, two seconds later, or if the ball is already out in the parking lot. If it's a touchdown, it will still be a touchdown when he raises his arms.

Patience is a learned virtue for officials. Pay attention to NFL officials and experienced college officials. Odds are they will calmly call a touchdown. College officiating wasn't that way fifteen or twenty years ago. Officials back then were into the game and were excited about making calls. I've worked with guys who literally jumped off the ground when signaling a touchdown, and I've never understood why. Officials who work games without emotion or wasted motion create a sense of confidence around them that when they have to make a tough call, everyone can feel that it's the right call.

Officials must rely on each other. Things happen so fast in a college football game, and sometimes only one person sees it. Other times, two or three of us see it. When we work with the same people week after week on a really good crew, we become comrades, and we come to each other's aid if we have a problem. That's a drawback of split crews and swing crews. Officials working with two or three guys having a tryout will not lead to that same kind of camaraderie. Each official is trying to preserve his own career at that level. It's a small window for most guys, and if they can't make solid calls, they're not going to last. Hopefully, others on the crew won't hang a fellow official out to dry, but it does happen.

I worked the Texas–Baylor game in 1992, and it included the most controversial play I ever had where I totally blew it. Baylor was a huge underdog in head coach Grant Teaff's last game in Waco, but the Bears were winning and needed an important first down. A Baylor receiver ran a twelve-to-fifteen-yard hook pattern, and the pass was thrown right to him. He was hit at the same time the ball arrived and was being driven back downfield; his back was to me as I was coming down the sideline. I thought it was a catch, but could not see the ball. So I moved up the sideline to the point where I judged catch, moved in to the spot, and looked for help from the back judge, umpire, or anyone who could see the ball. My spot gave Baylor a first down. What I didn't see was the ball dribbling out, meaning the receiver never had possession. Of course, I thought the receiver dropped it after the Texas players pushed him back. The side judge, back judge, umpire, and referee all saw it, but no one said a word. I ruled first down as a result of forward progress. With the first down, Baylor was able to run out the clock and score a major upset of the Longhorns.

I was watching ESPN in my hotel room that night, and there I was right where an official never wants to be, in the game highlights, or lowlights, as officials call them. The camera angle from the other side of the field clearly showed the receiver never had the ball. What followed was an interview with Texas athletic director DeLoss Dodds, who said, to his credit, officials make bad calls just like the rest of us. But my name was mud in Austin the next week. It was one of those things I couldn't see. I would work the play the same way the rest of my career and be happy to have another official come to me and say, "The receiver did not have possession." We can simply rule incomplete and go back to the previous spot and play the next down. No harm done.

The larger point is that no one came to my aid on that crew, and I remember all those other officials to this day. To be fair, this wasn't my regular crew. For some reason, I was inserted into that crew for that particular game. I looked bad, but I'm not saying it wasn't my fault. I ruled a catch, but someone could have overruled me. Maybe no one else saw it. I have a hard time believing that. It was a low point for me, but a high point for Baylor coach Grant Teaff. It was his last game in Waco, and his team beat Texas. Funny thing, the Longhorns snapped it over their punter's head twice that day, gave up field position to the Bears when they should not have, but my poor call late provided them with a scapegoat to pin the loss on.

It takes passion and mental toughness to be an official. It requires a certain personality to officiate because there is no reason to do it beyond our love of the game. We don't get rich. We don't become famous. We do get second-guessed and ridiculed a lot. Successful officials love the game and give time to the game. Those who belong to high school officiating chapters work just as hard attending meetings each week beginning in August, are required to attend rules and mechanics clinics and are tested on their knowledge of the rules. They work scrimmages with more seasoned officials to learn how to officiate, and they're hardly compensated at all.

Something that distinguishes veteran officials from their less seasoned counterparts is comportment. How do we handle ourselves on the field? How do we react when the pressure is on? How are we perceived on the field?

One of the most satisfying things to me as far as my Division I career goes is that I flagged only one coach on the sideline. I never flagged a Division II coach for sideline antics. My philosophy was that I was on the sideline in a one-on-one situation with a coach and should be the liaison between the crew and that coach. If the only interpersonal skills I have are to flag a coach every time he gets under my skin, then something is wrong. I like to think I can take a lot of abuse. I tried to be calm and courteous while understanding that coaches are under a lot of pressure to win games. I prided myself in the fact that I could get along with coaches without having to threaten them with penalties.

If a coach was irate, I tried to answer his questions and then get away from him. Most of the coaches I worked with knew I had a high tolerance for their antics and the verbal thrashings they gave me as long as they never crossed the line and personally cussed me. We had one coach who did that the first time I ever worked his sideline. He was not well-liked by Big 12 officials. He was abusive, and maybe that was because he came into the league from the NFL. His attitude was he knew more than any official could possibly know. Some of the abuse he got away with was uncalled for.

I worked his sideline one afternoon at Iowa State when his team was the visitor. After I had made a perfectly correct call on the sideline that did not go his way, he said one of the magic words. He didn't have as good a look at the play as I did, but that didn't keep him from showering me with vulgarities. Instead of getting mad when he was in my face, I stood on the sideline until I'd heard all I wanted to hear. Then I calmly killed the clock, went out five steps, turned around and threw my flag for a fifteen-yard unsportsmanlike-conduct penalty against the bench.

That's when he came after me, but his coaches intercepted him and moved him down the sideline away from me. I continued to be amazed. He was coaching a storied program, and I thought to myself, "Why is this guy leading one of the premier programs in America?" I couldn't imagine why he was there. Turns out he isn't there any more.

Officials have to be aware that in this age of television and sports-talk entertainment, they are going to be scrutinized and critiqued more than ever before. Big 12 officials work important games week after week. League teams regularly appear on television in venues such as Notre Dame, Florida State, Nebraska, Texas, Oklahoma, Colorado, and Texas A&M. It is all about how we comport ourselves. How will fans, coaches, the television audiences, and the announcers perceive an official as far as how he walks, stands, gives signals, treats people, and his attitude. Little things make the difference. Some officials will make an incomplete pass signal while looking down at their feet, causing fans to wonder if he is ever going to stop. The more seasoned officials will plant their feet with their head up looking out where the play occurred, give the signal in no more than three waves, turn around, and walk off. That's the difference, and it's all about presentation.

That's something we heard about all the time. Every time I went to a summer meeting, I heard about presence on the field, looking sharp, each crew member wearing the same kind of shoes, making sure those shoes were shined, and that we kept flags in our pockets where they couldn't be seen. Officials should walk with confidence.

I walked to my position with purpose. No one in the stadium was there to see me, and no one cared how fast I could run to my position. All that mattered was that I was in the right position at the right time and used good judgment. Everyone else at that game should be able to tell I'd been there before. When I see players score a touchdown and then move into some celebration, I wonder if it's the first time they've ever been in the end zone. Players should give credit to the teammates who helped get them there. Let's be clear here: Officials understand the difference between youthful exuberance—a natural part of the game—and a choreographed "all about me" demonstration, which is not part of the game. Football is a team sport, and players do not get into the end zone without a lot of help.

The supervisor of officials is constantly reminding his officials that Big 12 football is the big time, and we have to act like it. We can't show up with scuffed shoes, our shirttails hanging out, a sweat-stained hat, and our bellies hanging out. We must look like we're part of the game and not just someone who was dragged out of the stands. Should you have to tell officials that? No, but like anything else, it is repetition, and the more often it is done right, the quicker it becomes habit.

It's the same thing as seeing enough snaps to know when a defensive player is moving at the line and trying to make an offensive lineman jump. An experienced official can tell if the defensive player was doing something related to football, such as shifting down the line or resetting a stance, or faking a start, which is a defensive foul.

We don't watch the snap and *think* the player was offsides, because the ball has been snapped and handed off by that time. We don't have the luxury of time. We have to have done it enough times where if something is wrong, we *know* it. The result is an immediate flag. We have to overcome a tendency to think rather than react early in our careers if we are to be successful.

Basketball officials work with a whistle in their mouths. Football officials carry the whistle. I carried mine in my left hand. My right hand was free to throw the flag if needed. I wasn't born with the ability to run around carrying a whistle in my left hand or to whip out a flag and throw to the correct spot all the while never taking my eyes off my keys. In basketball, if a play is whistled dead, it's rarely a big deal. In football, if we blow a play dead at the wrong time, we've messed up the game. By carrying the whistle in my hand, I've saved myself from making huge mistakes many times with inadvertent whistles due to the short time span it takes for the whistle to get to my mouth. For us, it's a matter of seeing thousands of snaps and being able to do things as a natural reaction over and over again.

Many coaches fail to realize that an official's lack of concentration is sometimes a result of the coach not leaving the crew alone to work the game. There are times when they need to say something to us, but they need to coach the rest of the time. I have never understood why so many coaches have felt the need to be so vocal about officiating when they are doing so many things wrong on the coaching side. A coach will usually tell you that they had some bad calls during the season, and some will also tell you they had bad calls that went in their favor. By the end of the year, those calls usually tend to balance out. That is no justification for bad calls; that's just the way the game works.

Understanding situations is another important part of comportment. We try to teach young officials to call holding at the fifty-yard line the same way they would call it at the ten-yard line. If it's holding at the fifty, don't wait until the team gets to the ten to call it. That's hard to teach. Having a grasp of the game is important. One can't just be a black-and-white rules guy; officials have to understand the situation. That provides consistency, which is what coaches, players, and fans are looking for.

Officials should walk around that field looking as relaxed during the final two minutes of the game as they did at the opening kickoff.

An official who took me on his crew in Division II years ago, Jim Schiermeyer, had two quotes he used all the time. One was that he wasn't looking for holding, but if it was shown to him, he was going to call it. The other one was it is a lot easier to shoot a rabbit standing still than from a moving horse.

I always tried to remember that someone who knows officiating was probably watching me when I officiated. When I put the flag down, I didn't want to look nervous about it. The rap on one of the other major conferences is that the officials in that league carried two yellow flags, both hanging clearly out of their back pockets. I kept mine out of sight, just as my league mandated. That's comportment. When you see officials with flags hanging out of every pocket, what does that say? "We're ready to throw." We prided ourselves in the Big 12 on not showing the yellow. We were not there to intimidate anyone. Officiating is a privilege, and we needed to remember that we were privileged to be there. The higher the level you work, the more important comportment becomes.

Comportment is even more important in this age of instant replay, which has brought another level of scrutiny to the college game. I disagree with replay being used in the college game, which, I thought, achieved a high level of appeal and popularity without it. Players make mistakes during plays, but we don't get to replay the down. Coaches make mistakes, but they don't receive another chance until the next play. Officials are part of the human element of the game, which is what makes it all that it is today. Have there been cases in which replay has helped? Absolutely. However, more times than not, the call is confirmed, and few times is a call overturned that impacts the game.

Instant replay, in essence, has opened Pandora's box. We now have another level where a chance of mistake exists. Consider the game early in the 2006 season between Oklahoma and Oregon in which the on-field and replay officials made errors on an onside kick in the game's final 1:12. Oregon scored two touchdowns in the waning moments to claim a 34–33 win. That was human error at the replay level. No matter what is done, it creates more room for second-guessing. College football became a great game without replay. As it is today, the system is imperfect. The replay official has to wait on television, and if there is no television, the in-house video system, to provide the correct feeds to make a call, and it all has to be done before the next play. If something appears suspect, the game is stopped and the wait begins, which takes time.

Replay has, to an extent, caused officials to change the way they officiate. Once an official rules a player down, that play is over. That's the way it's always been. Now, officials won't rule anyone down. If the ball is out (fumbled), they keep playing. Replay probably has made officials a little gun-shy. I worked games before replay, and I worked games after replay, and I worked games as a replay official. From my point of view, I think the replay system as it stands today in college football is a flawed system.

Who will serve as a replay official? Mostly former officials, guys who can't work on the field, and retired guys like me. If I wanted to continue to travel and jump through all the hoops it would take to be a replay official, I'd prefer to officiate on the field. Yes, the NFL has instant replay, but their system is superior. That league has spent a lot of money on it and pro football is a different game played by a different caliber of player. The college replay system relies heavily on television. If it's a game with a lower profile, the system relies on a few cameras in the stadium. The feeds throughout college football are not consistent. Each venue is different, and every broadcast is different. I've been in the replay booth before when we needed a better angle and couldn't get it because the feeds coming back to the booth were purely dependant on what the producer sent.

While it will never be a perfect system, it does seem to have gotten better each season since 2004. As replay progresses, it will improve. The system will be better this year than it was two years ago, but college football does not yet have a system where an official, the referee, can see the replays live on the sideline and make the call because that is a money issue. The college system depends on the man in the booth. I think if we have a guy willing to give up three days of his life every week to travel with a crew but not be on the field, I have to wonder why. If we're going to have a replay system, let's work toward one where the guy on the field sees the replays. Let him make the calls. Right now, it's a second-rate system.

Tragically, I think the decision to incorporate instant replay into officiating has taken some of the human element out of the game, and it's that human aspect that has helped college football become so great and entertaining.

Perhaps college football has lost some of its comportment?

What's the Call?

First and ten for Team A at its own twenty-yard line. Wide receiver (Player No. 88) catches a pass at the fifty and carries the ball across Team B's goal line for a touchdown. Officials flag No. 88 for illegal touching after he apparently stepped on the sideline at his own thirty-eight prior to the catch. It is possible that No. 88 was blocked out of bounds by the defender. What is the ruling with regard to instant replay?

A. A reviewable play regarding whether Player No. 88 contacted the sideline.

B. A reviewable play regarding whether Player No. 88 was blocked out of bounds.

C. A non-reviewable play.

(See page 196 for answer.)

CHAPTER TEN:
FANS, YOU GOTTA LOVE 'EM

"If you don't learn to laugh at trouble, you won't have anything to laugh at when you are old."

— Will Rogers

ONE GREAT THING about being an official is that it's possible to make every single fan mad, unintentionally or otherwise, by the time you leave. What I try to remember about fans and what makes them humorous to me is that I appreciate the fact each fan is 100 percent partisan. Fans see things one way and only one way. Rarely will you find a fan that will admit or agree that a call was good if it went against the fan's team.

If you understand that from an officiating point of view—that those people are not personally attacking you because they do not know you personally—you can appreciate the humor of the situation, whatever it might be.

Football is unlike a lot of other situations because it can be so serious and so tense, but looking back at the game a few days or weeks or even years later, we can laugh about things we thought were deathly serious at the time. I recently had a conversation with former Texas Tech head coach Spike Dykes, and we were laughing about a game I officiated for him years before. He was upset about a couple of calls I made then, but now we laugh about it. At least, I hope he was laughing for real.

We officials often enjoy the creative names and taunts the fans throw our way. We enjoy laughing at and talking about what we were called from week to week. On my crew we had an ongoing contest to see who could tell us a new one that either they themselves had been called or one they had overheard. Spadeface, zebra breath, and zebra droppings are some of the more modern titles we hold.

I remember working a game between Seminole and Cooper, a couple of Class 3A West Texas high school teams, and I had one player's mom follow me off the field. We had a play in a close game in which Cooper had the ball and was driving for what would have been the winning touchdown. It was fourth down, and Cooper called a running play. I was the referee. Cooper ran the ball toward the first-down marker, but Seminole tackled the ball carrier short of the yardage needed. Then, a Seminole player crashed in and hit the runner late.

I'd blown the whistle, and there was no doubt it was a late hit. So we flagged the player. Fans saw the ball was clearly short of the first down marker, and they thought we were going to add fifteen yards on top of the yardage gained. The rulebook, however, is clear. The ball is dead, and the possession is over. The fifteen-yard walkoff takes place *after* the change of possession. Seminole took the ball after the penalty, ran out the clock, and won the game.

As I was walking off the field toward the dressing room, one player's mother chased me down and tore into me verbally.

"I can't believe you cheated those sixteen-year-old kids," she exclaimed. "How does it feel to be a grown man and cheat kids like that?"

The last thing I wanted was a protracted conversation with a mom who probably didn't know the rules. That's the kind of incident you just have to ignore and walk away from. I don't appreciate being accused of cheating young men. I played the game. When we are accused of that, our integrity is being attacked. It's one thing to be called blind, partial, incompetent, or whatever. You expect some of that, and it gives you pause.

From that encounter on, I tried to remember that anything a fan said was coming from a completely partisan viewpoint. Unfortunately, officials have to always be on their guard walking through a crowd after the game, whatever level it might be. You just never know how seriously someone is taking the game.

I'm always uncomfortable going through a crowd with the stripes on. At the high school level, security was not a big issue, especially more than twenty years ago when I was working those games. However, one game in particular still stands out. I worked a 1984 second-round playoff game between Post and Littlefield—a couple of perennial West Texas high school powers. Both teams were good, and Littlefield was able to pull out a 14–6 victory in a game that lived up to its advance billing.

For that week, it was *the* game in the area, and the crew I was part of went to Post to call the game. I was living in Morton at the time, so I drove to Lubbock and rode with the crew. We wanted to have a good pregame meeting. Kickoff was at 7:30 PM, so we planned to be at the game site about 5:30, and we arrived a little before that. When we pulled up to park near the stadium, people were already lined up waiting to get into the game.

We now had to walk through that crowd with our suitcases to get into the stadium, and it was pretty obvious to everyone who we were. A couple of hours later, when game time rolled around, we went from our dressing room in the fieldhouse near the stadium through the chain-link fence to get onto the field. It was, literally, standing room only all around that field. We didn't have an escort or anything like that. In West Texas, we didn't feel a lot of anxiety about that kind of situation, but that was my first case of being around a large crowd and walking through fans while wearing the stripes.

In this case, West Texas hospitality won out over fan hostility and nothing ugly happened. A crowd of that size was a rarity for the high school games I typically worked. But at the college level? That's another story.

I once worked a game at Arkansas in 1989, and our crew stayed at a hotel in downtown Little Rock. We dressed at the hotel. We like doing that because it keeps us from having to get into the stadium and worry about dressing there. More times than not the accommodations that serve as official's dressing rooms are a star or two below five. We held our pregame in a great meeting room at the hotel and went down to the hotel lobby to wait for our ride. Arkansas sent a van, more commonly called a paddy wagon, with bars on the windows and driven by two police officers.

To drive up to the stadium, our driver had to maneuver through the crowd. The van pulled up next to the stadium fence where a gate was open. We stepped out of the van right into the stadium. That's how close we were. We had an eventful game that day, and the Razorbacks wound up losing a close one. No sooner had the game ended than we hopped back into the paddy wagon to leave.

Some of the Arkansas faithful, angry because their team had lost and looking for someone to blame it on other than players and coaches, made our exit interesting. They grabbed the bars on the windows and started shaking the vehicle. Having a police escort made us feel safer. We figured the police would make them stop, but they told us they weren't about to venture out into that crowd. You can imagine how a vehicle responds in a crowd of walking people; the crowd has the advantage. This crowd was unhappy about the game and even unhappier with us. We didn't know if we were going to get out of there or not. To me, that's part of the college football spectacle, albeit not a pretty part.

Officials are taught to get off the field and to the dressing room immediately after a game. The first thing I always did was take my whistle off because I once saw a guy grab an official's lanyard. When that happens, that person has control. If a crowd was around me, I also took my hat off because people were bad about grabbing an official's hat. If they did that, what could we do? We were in the middle of a crowd, unpopular and outnumbered.

I believe the prudent course of action is to get out of there. No good can ever come from an official hanging around after a game. One team has lost, and someone, somewhere is upset about a call.

The best thing we can do is get off the field and get into our street clothes as quickly as possible. Fans won't even recognize us once the stripes are off. In fact, we enjoy going into coffee shops after the game and asking how the game went. When fans don't recognize us, we express a less jaded view of the game. I've done that before when I could tell people had just been to a game. I would strike up a conversation with them. "Did you go to the game?" "How was it?" Sometimes the answer is something like, "The officials really screwed up." Sitting there asking questions gave us a chance to play dumb, like we were in town on business.

But I've left settings like that when everyone in the place was mad, and the answer to our questions was something like, "We won in spite of the officials."

I worked a game between Texas and Houston that was nationally televised by ESPN during the 1990 season. The Cougars were ranked third in the country. At that time, John Jenkins was the head coach, and his team, led by quarterback David Klingler, was beating everybody by wide margins. In fact, this game marked the first time Houston had been picked to beat Texas easily. The Longhorns weren't exactly struggling, either. They were ranked No. 14 in the country, but the unbeaten Cougars were flying high.

What happened? Texas played an inspired game and won. The Longhorns, behind quarterback Peter Gardere and running back Butch Hadnot, got Houston down 28–10 by halftime and even the least knowledgeable fan could tell who was going to win the game. Texas built a 45–10 lead before Houston scored a couple of meaningless touchdowns in the fourth quarter of a 45–24 UT win. The Cougars' final score came with twenty-four seconds remaining, and that sizeable crowd realized the home team was going to win. The fans started pouring onto the sideline. When I looked up after the Cougars' extra-point try was good, I was amazed. There were as many people around the sideline as there were in the stands. The field looked like a river of people.

We were trying to get ready for the ensuing kickoff, and we had to go up and down the sideline moving people back. Fans just flooded the field after the kickoff return. Texas got the ball back, and the field was flooded with people again. We still had less than thirty seconds to play, but we had no way to get the fans off the field. From an official's point of view, few things are as repulsive as an inebriated college student. At this point, I was really worried. I took my hat and lanyard off, and my only thoughts were of my own safety. I was wondering how I could get to the west side of the stadium and negotiate the steps down to our dressing room without getting mauled.

I took a unique approach. I found a huge Texas player, got behind him and followed him to the sideline. That was one of the few times I was really concerned about someone trying to steal my hat, take my flag, or grab my whistle. If an official is knocked down in that setting, it could be tragic. I still remember a game in Lubbock between Texas Tech and Texas A&M. The crowd rushed on to the field, and some guy chased an official and pushed him down from behind. In that case, the official got up and went after the guy who pushed him, but in a crowd of that size it's total chaos, even with a healthy contingent of law enforcement personnel around. Fortunately, I never had anyone come after me like that.

Working Division I football is different from the other levels in many ways, but one primary difference is security. I always felt less secure in the small-college setting, but that could be a false perception. When I officiated those games, I would look around and see maybe one or two guys in uniforms in the entire stadium. This was almost thirty years ago, and a greater emphasis is placed on security today. Big 12 member schools are sensitive about security, which is why they do not want fans on the field.

No one ever knows what might happen in a college football game. I worked a game once that featured a bench-clearing brawl between Eastern New Mexico University and Texas Lutheran. Anytime you have fifty or sixty players in the middle of a field fighting, a couple of local law enforcement members will have a hard time breaking it up, so don't expect officials to get in the middle of something like that. We're not putting our lives in jeopardy. If representatives from the home school cannot control a situation like that, what's going to happen if a fan comes after one of us for what was perceived to be a missed call?

I noticed a lot of good players in the Division II league I worked. My perception was that many of those players could have been Division I players except for the baggage they were carrying, such as academic issues, that prevented them from playing at a higher level. They were good players who played tough football, but many were undisciplined, and no one knew when one of those guys might come uncoiled at an official.

Make no mistake. They have some great coaches and some great programs at that level. I'm not trying to take anything away from anybody. That level is where I learned to work at a greater speed because it's a faster game than the high school level. It might not be

Division I football, but the players are tougher, harder hitting, and run more sophisticated sets than we had in prep games. Division II is a training ground for officials. Like anything else, some officials come out of those leagues and move on, and others do not.

The Lone Star Conference, a small-college league with teams in Texas, New Mexico, and Oklahoma, is a tough league to work. Officials get the abuse and all that goes along with that. I don't think officials at the Big 12 level mind because working at those schools is a reward and privilege. It's hard to hang around a long time for abuse in Edmond, Oklahoma; Abilene, Texas; and Blackwater Draw, New Mexico.

Another place we run into fans is on the sideline. Hangers-on populate every college football sideline in America. From my position on the wing, that can be tough. When those teams break the huddle, I am totally focused on the play. If I have some loudmouth behind me talking about calls I made, it's a distraction. Those people are the worst. They were right behind me, and I could not look around to do anything about it because I had more important things to do. If a number of people were back there, I had no idea who it was mouthing off.

I put up with that for a long time until I figured out a technique to handle it. After a play was over, I'd turn around and say, "Do you want to say that to my face now that I can look at you? If you're not going to say it to my face, don't say it to my back." Generally, that would shut them up. I believe if a fan wants to bad-mouth me, fine, but do it from the stands. Down here on the sideline, the only person who gets that privilege is the head coach. I didn't believe in taking guff from assistant coaches, either. If one was on me, I usually went to the head coach and said, "Make him shut up or I can make him shut up." Usually, when confronted, no one says anything. The other part is if I had someone doing that on the sideline, it wouldn't bother me in the least to put them in the stands. That's where the fans are. On the field, they don't get to say anything.

I once had a guy on the Iowa State sideline riding me pretty hard. I turned around and gave the speech, but he kept it up. I responded by asking a university police officer to put the guy in the stands. The officer wouldn't do it. He said it wasn't his job.

The same thing happened on the sideline of a game I worked at the old Pitt Stadium on campus. Texas was playing the Panthers, and Johnny Majors was the Pitt coach. A guy was on my case something fierce. He was cussing me like no one's business. I turned around and figured out who it was. I asked the police to put him in the stands, and they escorted him off the sideline. I didn't think anything else about it until halftime. One of the Pitt ball boys said he was glad I did it because the guy acted like that every week. He said I was the first official ever to make him leave and sit in the stands. I was curious why no one had done anything about it before. He said I had ejected Coach Majors' brother.

Thankfully, we don't hear everything. We certainly don't hear it while the game is in progress. Before kickoff, if some guy is wising off, that's one thing. During timeouts, we can hear them. After a touchdown, if I'm standing down in the end zone during a TV timeout and someone is insulting me, I hear some of that. If it's bad, the best thing to do is walk to the middle of the field. The professional official ignores it.

The fan is not personally attacking me; he or she is attacking the stripes. Take the stripes off, and those same fans will treat me like anyone else if they don't know I'm an official. They are just fans who pay their money, which I believe entitles them to holler at officials and coaches from the stands. I don't think they should be on the players; those are college kids not being paid to play. Players are doing the best they can under the circumstances. I don't think fans ever have a reason to berate a college player. They have bad days and don't play as well as they can. That's part of the game.

That goes back to my philosophy about not flagging many coaches. Ultimately that's penalizing the players on the field. I believe in going great lengths to get along with people and always felt like if I had to resort to flagging a coach for something that happened on the sideline, that wasn't the best approach. Those players are out on that field paying with a physical beating to their bodies to gain a yard and an official on the sideline takes fifteen of those yards away because he can't tolerate some abuse on the sideline? I'm not saying I didn't do it, but I did go to great lengths not to do it for that reason. I have too much respect for the game and the teams on the field to let outside matters interfere.

The line that cannot be crossed, though, is when an official is personally attacked with profanity. Is there a lot of profanity used on the sidelines? Yes, but that's part of the game. When someone says you are a sorry S.O.B., that's crossing the line, but if they say that was a sorry S.O.B. call, that's another thing because, hey, they might have been right.

Second-guessing my judgment never bothered me. I figured I was wrong sometimes, but I was right a whole lot more. The filming and grading sessions after a game ultimately told me if I was right or wrong, but for someone to attack me personally and use profanity in the process was out of bounds.

Want to see the opposite approach? When you compare what we take as football officials to what baseball umpires take, it's basically 180 degrees away. Umpires do not take anything from anybody, and participants don't have to say much to get thrown out of the game. I've never understood that mentality.

With basketball officials in a gym, fans see what's going on. In football, it's different. Fans don't see what goes on all the time on the sideline from one end to the other. The only officials immune to it are the referee, the umpire, and the back judge because they are in the middle of the field and don't have to listen to it. I made my career on the sideline. Part of that is interacting with the people on the sideline.

Rarely do officials receive any trash talk from players. As a whole in college football today, coaches teach their players not to talk to officials. A player might ask a question, and if it's asked in the right vein, he will get an answer. Officials love to talk to players when appropriate.

When I talk to younger officials, I counsel them not to have rabbit ears. That is what gets officials into trouble. We have to let negative remarks roll off our backs, even if a coach is on us all afternoon. When it's time to report a foul, maybe that foul is called on the other side of the field. The official has to walk up to that coach, look him in the eye, and communicate the call to him in a professional manner. Let the coach's comments go, and when it's time to talk to a coach, talk to him.

Fans, though, are a different breed, and they are unique. I think fans are tougher in certain places than others. The fans at the Orange Bowl, where I worked a regular-season game for Miami, seemed to be vicious. They spat on us as we came out of the tunnel—and that was before the game. I'm sure they treated all officials that way. You can't take it personally. That was part of the atmosphere there at that time. It was a fairly tough place to officiate.

Overall, the fans of marquee programs are sophisticated and intelligent. I think if someone were to conduct a poll of Big 12 officials, they would tell you Nebraska supposedly has the most hospitable fans. They will boo if they don't like a call, but I don't remember any hateful comments coming out of the stands there, not that I listened for them. They seemed to be the most appreciative fans. When I worked games there, they clapped for the opposing team. Of course, they were winning then, but they seemed to appreciate a good ball game. One of the most hospitable places I worked was Texas A&M. The people there were always respectful. Texas fans at Memorial Stadium are another story. That's a tough crowd.

My experience is I could always tell a stadium where alcohol was being sold based on fan behavior. We had few venues in the Southwest Conference and the Big 12; in fact, usually it was only when a college game took place in a professional facility such as the Astrodome in Houston. The most visible example of this that I recall occurred in the 1999 season opener between Colorado and Colorado State at Denver's Mile High Stadium.

Colorado State routed the Buffaloes 41–14 in a venue that offered alcohol sales. With two minutes remaining, the game administrator came to me on the sideline and said, "As soon as this game is over with, get your crew off the field immediately. We think there's going to be trouble." With one minute left, the Denver riot police, wearing gas masks and shields, encircled the field facing the stands in an effort to keep the Colorado State student body from coming onto the field and tearing down the goalposts. The Denver Broncos were scheduled to play a home game the next day.

Before we could get off the field once time expired, the Denver police were firing tear gas and pepper spray into the stands. I don't know why they were doing this, but the smell of smoke and gas was everywhere. It was well over an hour before we could leave our dressing room following the game. My assumption is this incident had something to do with alcohol being served.

The thing to remember is the football field is a fantasy world that's hard to break away from. You take a look at it and realize it's not going to last. No matter how good an official is, no matter how good a league is, no matter how many great games you get to work, it's going to come to an end. That requires an adjustment. It's a high to be on that field in the middle of coaches, players, and fans on a Saturday afternoon. And it was one heck of a ride and privilege that I enjoyed every time I put on the stripes.

What's the Call?

Team A's punter (No. 36) intends to punt from his own end zone on fourth down and ten from his own five-yard line. He catches the snap but fumbles it prior to the kick. Team A No. 42 picks the ball up and runs the ball out to the twenty for a first down. What is the ruling?

A. First down for A at the twenty.

B. Touchback for A, first and ten at the twenty.

C. Safety, award Team B two points.

(see page 196 for answer.)

Afterword

OFFICIATING IS A matter of pride, passion, and commitment. Those men fans see on the field, by the time they are merely being considered to become Division I college football officials, understand what the job requires in terms of sacrifice and what it will not deliver in terms of recognition.

They spend a lot of time away from their families. They invest, literally, hundreds of hours in training to be qualified and competent just to set foot on that field. And they do all of this for something they love.

A good official never goes out there thinking about the last play. He doesn't have any predetermined thoughts about officiating the game. A good official simply prepares himself to go out and do his best to keep the playing field level where neither team is afforded an unfair advantage. An official completely understands how important each game is, not just how it fits in the national situation or the respective conference race, but how important that game is to each individual kid on the field, each parent, and each fan sitting in the stands.

That's because officials have been players or fans themselves during their life prior to becoming an official. They have a tremendous amount of respect for the game and for those talented players. An official quickly realizes—despite believing he is God's gift to officiating—it was he who blew a handful of calls in that peewee game he just worked. Humbling experiences such as those provide officials with an early perspective on exactly how much will be required from them in this avocation.

Division I football is really just a small step down from the National Football League. Officials at that level have to get their eyes, body, on-field movements, and ability to make decisions honed to handle the game confidently and competently.

Officials are proud of what they do, but it takes special people to realize praise in this business will be rare. Someone loses every game, and every so often, the finger of blame is pointed at the officiating crew and close calls that were made one way but maybe would have helped the other team had they gone their way. When you analyze it, though, very seldom can anyone point to an officiating error that cost a team a game. Yes, it happens, but it is extremely rare. The ability to withstand that kind of scrutiny and second-guessing requires a strong internal commitment.

I worked for the Internal Revenue Service and have been married to the same woman for over forty-one years. That training as a husband and father of four, coupled with seventeen years of working for the IRS, conditioned me very well for never being right. The same approach has to be standard operating procedure for officials because for every 50,000 fans in a 100,000-seat stadium who thought that was a wonderful call, the other side and their 50,000 think it was a lousy call and that the official involved is an idiot. For their part, coaches are probably thinking the same thing; they're just not saying it (maybe).

That is unbelievable pressure to withstand, and it's something Mike Liner has captured quite well within the pages of this book. No one realizes better than Mike that officials have to be comfortable with what they are doing and have the personality to shut out all of the screaming, hollering, questioning, and blaming that occurs during the game and continues after the game. Once all the dust settles, officials know they did the best they could and accept the fact that they make mistakes that will give them a chance to learn and become even better officials. They have to live with the fact that a lot of given people in a college town are going to think they're crazy, but the official and the supervisor he's working for know deep down that isn't the case.

Their passion is apparent in other ways. The work an official does is not indicative of the compensation he receives. Mike spends time talking about this issue as well. Unfortunately, the passion that is a great asset for officials is also something of an albatross. They put everything aside to work a game they love, and consequently, management knows they would do it for free. While compensation for college officials has increased recently, I'm sure those who work the games wouldn't argue with anyone in favor of additional pay hikes.

Regardless, successful officials have a certain presence when they are on the field, and people can tell the ones who have it. If I could define what it is, I could probably make millions for the NFL and all the college conferences. Mike is a good example. When he worked his first game in the Southwest Conference, we harassed him a little bit like anyone else to see what kind of guy he was. But he had it, and I knew it when I saw it. The best way to describe it is a presence officials have on the field where fans, players, coaches, and fellow officials have confidence in an official and what he did to get to that level.

No matter the sport, officials won't receive many pronouncements about just how wonderful they are. No one is going to walk up to a microphone in the first quarter and say, "Those officials are really doing a great job today." The conference staff will provide those pats on the back, and not many of those, throughout the year, but basically, this is a job you never get thanked for by the hundreds of millions of people who watch it. Which is the way it should be. When it doesn't matter what the officials did, and it doesn't matter if one team wins and one team loses, that's when people will quit paying to come to the games.

Officials don't want to be thanked. Heck, they really don't even want to be noticed. They just want to do the best job they can that day and then work to do it better the next time.

And that's as black and white as it gets.

—Tim Millis
Executive Director,
NFL Referees Association

A Final Word from Mike

THANKS FOR TAKING the time to read my book. I've tried to give readers an entertaining look at life through the eyes of a college football official. It's a unique perspective and one I hope you have gained some insight into. As you can tell, officiating is something that has been special to me for a long time. Something else I consider special is my relationship with Buckner International, a non-profit multiservice organization dedicated to helping the lives of orphans and desperate children. The cause resonates with me so much that all proceeds from *It's Not All Black and White* will go directly to the Buckner Foundation, which supports the work of Buckner International. So, thanks again for reading, and thanks for lending a helping hand to a worthwhile organization. For more information on the vision and mission of Buckner, visit www.buckner.org

—Mike Liner
December 19, 2008
Lubbock, Texas

Answers to What's the Call?

1. B. Touchback. Rule 8-6-1-A.

2. B. Safety, award Team B two points. Rule 8-7-2-A.

3. C. Offensive pass interference. Rule 7-3-8-a.

4. D. Ineligible man downfield, penalize five yards from previous spot. Rule 7-3-10.

5. C. Safety, Rule 8-7-2-A.

6. C. Award Team A two points. Rule 8-3-2-d-1.

7. A. Touchback. Rule 8-6-1-A.

8. A. No contact by Team B player, so pass ruled incomplete. Rule 7-3-9-f.

9. A. Reviewable regarding whether Player No. 88 contacted the sideline. Rule 12-3-1-c.

10. C. Safety, award Team B two points. Rule 8-7-2-A.

* *Source: 2008 NCAA Football Rules and Interpretations*

Acknowledgments

"Officials are the only guys who can rob you and then get a police escort out of the stadium."

—Ron Bolton

IT'S SUZIE'S FAULT, but don't blame her. If it weren't for my wife, the book you hold in your hands never would have happened. She deserves the credit. Without her constant encouragement, steady support, and occasional nagging, I could not have finished writing it. She stayed after me, and I can't thank her enough for that.

Between her and my writer, Doug Hensley, I didn't really have a chance. Each believed in the project more than I did. Doug, who now works for The Dollins Group, approached me about the project, encouraged me to explore it, and then spent countless hours with me breathing life into the pages of this book. Forget the fact that we've been friends for a long time; he brought a unique perspective into this relationship. With two decades of sportswriting under his belt, he understood something about officials and the demands they face. He brought great insight and was the steady hand I needed. When I was discouraged about the book, he was there to keep me from throwing my hands up and turning my back on the whole thing. This book was not simply thrown together. It is the result of a full year of effort. Doug's vigilance and perseverance were assets this banker could always count on.

No one ever realizes his or her true potential without a lot of help from a lot of people. This is no less true in the world of the college football official. Think about it: Seven guys in a stadium running around in striped shirts have no one to rely upon but each other for the better part of four hours. Each decision is guaranteed to spark a reaction of some kind from at least half of the crowd.

I've been blessed to work with a number of great officials at the high school, small college, Southwest Conference, and Big 12 levels. Many of those men have had a profound influence on my officiating career. Many of these are mentioned within the pages of this book, but I would be remiss if I didn't take a moment to thank some of those men for what they've meant to me. Ronnie Freeman, Jake Webb, Ray O'Brien, the late Billy Ledbetter, and the late Jay Lindsey were superb high school officials whom I hold in high regard.

SWC officials I enjoyed working with included Max Smithey, Bo Hicks, Bud Alexander, Larry Weeks, Lynn Lawhan, James Wilson, and the late Pancho Gerard. During my career, many of the Big 12 officials I have enjoyed working with through the years include Tim Crowley, Don Kapral, Tim Pringle, Randy Christal, Tom Walker, and the late David Alexander.

Thanks to Rogers Redding and Tim Millis for agreeing to write the foreword and afterword, respectively. I look at this book as the literal final chapter of my officiating career. It seems only right that two men who were early influences on me as a college football official, Rogers and Tim, provide wonderful bookends that reflect the passion and respect I have for the culmination of a lifelong avocation. Rogers has an incredible collection of football officiating experiences that have influenced and impacted officials across the country. Tim was the first supervisor of officials for the Big 12 Conference, and he is one of the greatest commonsense football officiating minds ever to come along.

The guys who work college football games are unlike anyone else in that they have a job that requires perfection every week and improvement the next week. Is that realistic or fair? No, but that's the expectation.

Understanding that is one thing. Dealing with it is another thing entirely, but I was fortunate that a number of people took an interest in seeing me succeed as a football official, and this work would not have been possible without their assistance. I'd like to take a moment to thank them.

The late Jim Schiermeyer gave me the chance to begin my college football officiating career by having me work on his Lone Star Conference crew all those years ago. He was the referee of a six-man crew in those days, and I was one of the five other guys who made up his crew.

Clint Ramsey had a huge influence on my career. He was a Southwest Conference official with whom I worked occasionally at the high school level. Clint was nice enough to recommend me to the SWC when it was looking for an official from Lubbock.

Charlie Carraway was an SWC official who influenced me because he was a great line judge at the college level, and I admired the way he performed the job. Mechanically, he was superb, and I wanted to pattern myself after him.

Ken Faulkner, former longtime SWC supervisor of officials, gave me my first break. Ken had a long history of officiating, and he was on the NCAA Rules Committee. He had a tremendous impact on the game. Before he passed away, he was inducted into the College Football Hall of Fame for his officiating contributions.

Wendell Shelton came up through the officiating ranks and followed Ken as SWC supervisor of officials. He was a good official, and he took me on his crew my first full year in the SWC. The line judge from Wendell's crew, Walt Coleman, had moved on to the NFL, so he needed a line judge. We had a great crew and we drew a lot of important games between 1989–91. That sort of kick-started my career, being on a great crew with a big-name official. Three other officials on that crew, Gary Slaughter, Tommy Moore, and George Coleman, also went on to the NFL.

I could not have succeeded as well without my friend Richard Whittenburg. He is as good a college football official, regardless of position, as I have ever seen. Richard is a great rules guy with outstanding common sense. When he began in the SWC, he was a field judge, which was not his natural position. Then he moved to head linesman. He could do it, but it wasn't where he would thrive.

Richard wanted to be an umpire, so the Big 12 moved him to that position. When he got into his natural position, he was among the best college football umpires in America. He worked championship games, bowl games, and always graded out among the best in the league. Richard and I weren't always on the same crew, but we were put together in the Big 12 because Tim knew we were cohesive. Richard and I became personal friends. We traveled together, roomed together, and suffered through some tough days-after together. Those are the things that meld a friendship.

Richard and fellow official Jon Bible also were instrumental in helping with research for this book. Thanks also to David Jones, who assisted in rounding up the photos that appear on these pages, and to Ron Murphy for providing the cartoons that appear at the start of each chapter.

Those are some of the guys I worked with, but I also want to thank former Texas Tech football coach Spike Dykes. I don't think any coach had more influence on my career. He encouraged me when I was down. He and I had many conversations over the years, and I officiated his games in the Southwest Conference and Big 12. Not every official has the ability to sit down with a coach and talk about officiating philosophies. It was a huge benefit for me to have someone like Spike to talk to.

I close by thanking God for surrounding me with opportunities to influence others and people who have influenced me. Truly, through Him all things are possible.

Index